CurriCUlum Focus

Tudors

Michael and Barbara Temple

HOPSCOTCH EDUCATIONAL PUBLISHING

Curriculum Focus series

History

Famous Events
Famous People
Invaders
Toys
Tudors

Geography

Islands and Seasides
The Local Area

Science

Ourselves: Key Stage 1
Animals, Plants and Habitats: Key Stage 1
Materials: Key Stage 1

Published by Hopscotch Educational Publishing Ltd,
Unit 2, The Old Brushworks, 56 Pickwick Road,
Corsham, Wilts SN13 9BX
Tel: 01249 701701

© 2003 Hopscotch Educational Publishing

Written by Michael and Barbara Temple
Linked ICT activities by Michelle Singleton
Series design by Blade Communications
Illustrated by Jane Bottomley
Cover illustration by Virginia Gray
Printed by Clintplan Limited, Southam

Michael and Barbara Temple hereby assert their moral
right to be identified as the authors of this work in
accordance with the Copyright, Designs and Patents Act,
1988.

ISBN 1-904307-54-X

Contents

	Cross-curricular links	4
	Introduction	5
1	The Tudor family	6
2	Henry VIII	15
3	Henry VIII's six wives	25
4	Henry VIII's marriages	35
5	The Tudor rich	44
6	The Tudor poor	58
7	Making comparisons	70
8	Tudor exploration	80
9	Drake's voyage	91
10	Settlements in America	103
	Answers	114
	Glossary	115
	Useful resources	117

Cross-curricular links

Chapter	History SoW	Geography SoW	PSHE and Citizenship	Literacy Framework	Numeracy Framework	ICT SoW
1	Unit 7			Y3, Term 1, T13 Y3, Term 2, T17	Y3, 91, 93	3A 4D
2	Unit 7		Unit 8 Unit 10	Y3, Term 2, S2; T17		4A
3	Unit 7			Y3, Term 2, T8, T17 Y4, Term 1, T11		4A
4	Unit 7		Unit 8 Unit 10	Y3, Term 1, T23 Y3, Term 2, T17 Y4, Term 1, S1		3A 3E
5	Unit 8			Y3, Term 2, T14, T17	Y3, 89	4B
6	Unit 8			Y4, Term 1, T12		3A
7	Unit 8	Unit 19		Y4, Term 1, T24		4A
8	Unit 19	Unit 18		Y5, Term 1, T24		5D
9	Unit 19	Unit 18		Y5, Term 1, T24 Y6, Term 1, T17		3A 4A
10	Unit 19	Unit 18		Y5, Term 1, T24 Y6, Term 1, T17		6A

Introduction

Curriculum Focus: Tudors brings history alive for children and teachers alike. It provides the material and support needed to plan and teach interesting and informative lessons, and uses a variety of methods, including material for use on an interactive whiteboard. Chapters 1–7 are based on the QCA schemes of work for history at Key Stage 2, Years 3/4, and Chapters 8-10 are based on the schemes of work for Key Stage 2, Years 5/6. Each chapter equips you with the ideas, skills and knowledge to deliver the full range of Tudor history at this key stage.

This book gives a clear approach to teaching historical ideas and to planning work for your classes, including:

- detailed **Teachers' notes** giving background information on each topic and/or the concept to be taught
- fully illustrated **Generic sheets** offering a wealth of reusable resource material
- a **Lesson plan** full of ideas for introducing and developing the lesson
- photocopiable and differentiated **Activity sheets** to support individual and group work. (Activity sheet 1 is intended for children who need more support. Activity sheet 2 is for those children who can work independently and Activity sheet 3 is for more able children.)

The material is designed to be used flexibly, and not necessarily consecutively, with the whole class. You can adapt and develop each chapter as the lessons unfold and the children become absorbed in the subject.

Most children will have heard of Henry VIII, but few will have an understanding of his place and importance in the development of English history. This book sets out to place Henry within his Tudor family and to look at the cause and effect of his actions within his own society and within the wider realms of European history. One of the key features of this book is its emphasis on starting from the children's own experience and relating it to the facts of history, helping Henry and his wives to become 'real' people. The activities are varied in style and allow different experiences for the children to learn and discover for themselves. The teachers' notes are purposely detailed to provide as much relevant information as necessary with an overlap of detail throughout the first four chapters on Henry. Excellent illustrations and further information for you to use will be found through the recommended websites, which have been thoroughly researched. For example, bring history to life by accessing the Tudor portraits in the National Portrait Gallery, either for the whole class to view on an interactive whiteboard or for the children to find out for themselves in an ICT lesson. (Website addresses do change, so check the sites out before using them in a lesson.) Relevant places to visit are also listed in Useful resources on page 117.

Children all have an understanding of being rich and poor in their own world and it is from this starting point that this book takes them back in time to look at the social issues of Tudor times. Use of drama and subjective discussions can enhance the fictional stories set out in Chapters 5 and 6. The teachers' material provides the necessary facts to keep the subject on track. A good balance between social and political history is provided in these Key Stage 2 history lessons for Years 3–4. The comparison of Tudor times with life today for rich and poor people could provide much information and encourage reflection.

The late Tudor period was a time of discovery and exploration. Chapters 8–10 take older Key Stage 2 children on their own voyage of discovery, weaving social and political history together. Modern-day exploration is the starting point and leads to the children discovering more about life as a Tudor explorer. Emphasis is placed on two famous men, Drake and Raleigh, but time is also given to the general life of sailors and their travels.

Possibly the most interesting subject of the book is saved for Chapter 10. The attempts by the English to settle in America were fraught with difficulties. The teachers' notes provide details of the troubled Roanoke settlement, the study of which is required by the QCA schemes of work. The events of history can can lead to the possible events of the future – is there life on other planets? Is space exploration as important as Tudor exploration? These are great starting points for children in Years 5 and 6 to explore their own ideas and to begin to recognise how the lessons of history are relevant to today.

CHAPTER 1

The Tudor family

The house of Tudor

From 1485 to 1603 a royal family known as the Tudors ruled England (see Generic sheets 1 and 2 on pages 10 and 11). On 22 August 1485, a Welsh nobleman called Henry Tudor defeated King Richard III at the Battle of Bosworth Field. Richard was killed in the battle, and legend has it that the English crown fell off his head and rolled into a bush. One of Henry's men saw something glinting in the sunlight, found the crown and placed it on his master's head, crowning him Henry VII, King of England.

Henry came to the throne at a difficult time, as civil war had been raging for 30 years between the houses of Lancaster (red rose) and York (white rose). The English people were tired of these Wars of the Roses and wanted a strong king who would bring peace. Henry, a Lancastrian, tried to end the feuding by marrying Elizabeth of York, daughter of Edward IV. In doing so, he united the Lancastrians and Yorkists into a new 'royal house' – the Tudors. Henry VII's emblem, the Tudor rose, showed this union by incorporating both the red and white roses (see Generic sheet 1). (The inner petals were white and the outer ones red.)

The reign of Henry VII

From the very outset of his reign, Henry VII stamped his authority on the country. He put down rebellions successfully and forced the barons to obey the law. These men had become very rich and powerful during the Wars of the Roses and needed to be brought into line. Henry did this by banning their private armies, taxing them heavily and punishing them in the Court of the Star Chamber if they broke the law. Henry also supported trade and exploration.

The accession of Henry VIII

When Henry VII died in 1509, his son Henry VIII became king. He was a handsome, athletic, eighteen-year-old who preferred to leave matters of state to his ministers while he enjoyed eating, dancing and jousting. Yet, like his father, he remained very much in control.

Shortly after he came to the throne, Henry married Catherine of Aragon, daughter of the king of Spain. This had been Henry VII's wish before he died.

In 1516, Henry and Catherine had a daughter, Mary. Henry was disappointed as he desperately wanted a son. In 1527, Henry fell in love with Anne Boleyn. In the hope that she might give him a son, he decided to divorce Catherine and marry Anne.

However, he needed the Pope's permission. The Pope's refusal resulted in an argument between them. Henry disobeyed the Pope and in 1533 married Anne. He now became head of the English Church in place of the Pope. He pulled down the monasteries, sold their lands and kept their riches. He used the money for a war against France.

Henry's marriage to Anne did not go well, especially when she gave birth to a girl, Elizabeth. He quickly lost interest in Anne and in 1536 had her beheaded. Henry then married Jane Seymour, and in 1537 was blessed with a son, Edward. Unfortunately, Jane, his favourite wife, died shortly afterwards. Henry married three more times, but had no more children. His final wife, Catherine Parr, outlived him.

The child king – Edward VI

When Henry died in January 1547, his nine-year-old son became King Edward VI. He was not a healthy child though and in 1553 his health was getting worse. Edward's chief adviser, the Duke of Northumberland, persuaded the king to make a will, naming Edward's 16-year-old cousin, Lady Jane Grey, as the next queen. The duke wished to keep his power after Edward's death. When the king did die though, in 1553, the English people refused to accept Lady Jane as queen, calling instead for Edward's stepsister, Mary. Lady Jane Grey and the Duke of Northumberland were arrested. Lady Jane had reigned for only nine days. Northumberland was executed straight away and Lady Jane went the same way the following year.

Bloody Mary

Queen Mary, daughter of Catherine of Aragon, was Catholic, unlike her Protestant stepbrother, and when she came to the throne she did everything in her power to make England a Catholic country again. The Pope was restored as head of the English Church and Mary severely punished anyone who opposed her. Nearly 300 Protestants were burnt to death at the stake in less than three years because of their religious beliefs. Among them were not only high-profile figures, such as Archbishop Cranmer and Bishops Latimer and Ridley, but many ordinary people. For allowing these horrific deaths to take place, Mary gained the nickname 'Bloody Mary'. She made things even worse in 1554 when she married the Catholic Philip II of Spain. When Mary died in 1558, few mourned her death. In fact, the church bells rang out in celebration, a far cry from the expectations people had of her on her accession.

The Virgin Queen

England's next monarch, Elizabeth I, a Protestant, was to be the last member of the Tudor dynasty, for despite pressure from her many advisers to marry, she was to remain single. For the majority of Elizabeth's reign, therefore, her Catholic cousin, Mary Queen of Scots, was heir to the English throne. When the Scots turned Mary off her Scottish throne, she fled to England. As Mary was a potential threat to

Elizabeth, the queen had no option but to keep her prisoner for 19 years. Mary Queen of Scots was finally executed in Fotheringhay Castle on 8 February 1587, as she had become the centre of Catholic plots to assassinate Elizabeth.

For the first 30 years of Elizabeth's reign, England was at peace, although there was always the possibility of an attack from Spain. The Catholic Mary Queen of Scots' execution was the final straw as far as Philip II was concerned, and in 1588 he sent a huge fleet of ships, the Armada, to attack and hopefully conquer England. The English had smaller ships, but their guns were better and their commanders, Lord Howard, Sir Francis Drake and Sir John Hawkins, were among the greatest in Europe. The Spanish were no match, and with the weather against them, less than half of the Spanish fleet returned to port. England was saved.

The Elizabethan period was also a great time for drama, poetry and discovery. Men who we still remember today, such as William Shakespeare and Walter Raleigh, lived during Elizabeth's reign.

Elizabeth died in 1603 and so came to an end the great period of Tudor kings and queens. It was to be a Scottish king who would inherit the throne of England – James Stuart, son of Mary Queen of Scots.

The Tudor family

History objective (Unit 7)
• To locate the Tudors within the context of the history of Britain.

Resources

- Generic sheet 2 (page 11)
- Whiteboard or OHP
- Activity sheets 1–3 (pages 12–14)
- Scissors and glue

Starting points: *whole class*

Talk to the children about what their own timeline would look like. Discuss what year they were born and what year it is now. Demonstrate on a whiteboard or OHP how these dates set the beginning and end of individual timelines. Give each child a copy of the individual timeline from Generic sheet 2 and ask them to fill it in, asking such questions as:

- What year did you start nursery or playgroup?
- What year did you join Beavers/Rainbows/football club?
- What year did you start school?

Briefly discuss the results.

Draw the English history timeline from Generic sheet 2 on the whiteboard or enlarge it for the children to see. Ask the children what names they can read and what dates they can see. Talk about the family name of today's monarch.

Look at the Tudor timeline on Generic sheet 2 together. What is the family name? What dates can be seen? Use this opportunity to discuss the concept of centuries. How long ago did the Tudors reign? Using the teachers' notes, give small outlines of the individual Tudor monarchs choosing one key fact to pass on to the children.

Before going into the group activities, explain how to read a family tree, remembering that the dates start from the reign of the monarch, not their birth date. Show the children the Tudor family tree on Generic sheet 2 and ask them to find out who was married to whom, who was whose mother and who reigned when.

Tell the children that they are now going to make their own Tudor timeline.

Group activities

Activity sheet 1
This sheet is aimed at children who need more support. They are asked to cut out the pictures and names of the Tudor monarchs and stick them on the timeline in the correct place.

Activity sheet 2
This sheet is aimed at children who are more independent workers. They have to cut out the pictures and names of the Tudor monarchs, pair them up, and then stick them on the timeline in the correct place.

Activity sheet 3
This sheet is aimed at more able children. They have to cut out and put together the pictures and names of the Tudor monarchs. They have to find a picture of Elizabeth I to draw as the 'missing monarch'. They then have to stick the pictures and names on the timeline in the correct order and add the dates.

Plenary session

Ask the children who have completed Activity sheets 1 and 2 to tell the class the order of the Tudor monarchs. Record their answers on the board. Invite the children who completed Activity sheet 3 to add the dates. Can they work out how long each monarch reigned? How long was the longest reign? How long was the shortest reign? How long ago from today's year did Henry VIII reign? Point towards the next lesson, which focuses on Henry VIII.

Ideas for support

If children have difficulty following a timeline, ask them to look carefully at the numbers on the timeline. Explain that the numbers are gradually getting bigger. Ask them if they can see the same number on the timeline as in the monarch's dates.

The first date is the lower number and is the start of the monarch's reign. The last date is the year of their death, and the start of the next monarch's reign.

Less able children could make coloured cards from the pictures of the Tudors to help them to differentiate between the Tudor monarchs.

Provide pictures or access to the National Portrait Gallery's website to help children find an image of Elizabeth I for Activity sheet 3. (See Useful resources on page 117.)

Ideas for extension

Ask the children to paint their own portraits of the Tudor monarchs. Display these on a large timeline with the dates written in old-style script writing by the children. The whole display could be bordered with Tudor roses drawn or stencilled by the children.

Decorate the classroom windows with Tudor roses made from tissue paper. Tudor roses made from felt, fabric or embroidery could also be used to decorate the room.

Ask the children to write an extract from the diary of Henry VIII or another Tudor monarch.

Help the children to research and formulate their own Tudor timeline to include more historical facts from the period. Encourage them to devise their own ways of presenting the information.

More able children could find out more about the monarchs who came before and after the Tudors. Ask why the Tudors came to power and why the Stuarts succeeded them.

Linked ICT activities

Using the internet and other resources, work with the children to find any information and pictures of Henry VII, Henry VIII, Edward VI, Mary I and Elizabeth I. Check with your LEA guidelines on children using search engines before asking the children to search the internet. Using a word processing or desktop publishing program such as *Textease*, Microsoft *Publisher* or Microsoft *Word* (see Useful resources on page 118), create a fact file about the Tudor monarchs. Create a template for the children to complete, using headings such as the year they were born, the year they died, the year they became king or queen, a description of their character, a description of their appearance.

Show the children how to copy and paste an image of the person from an internet site to accompany the text they have produced.

The children could work in groups of five, each member of the group researching information on a different monarch.

The completed fact files could be printed out, providing each group with their own facts about the Tudors. The fact files could be compiled together and placed in the class display.

The Tudor family

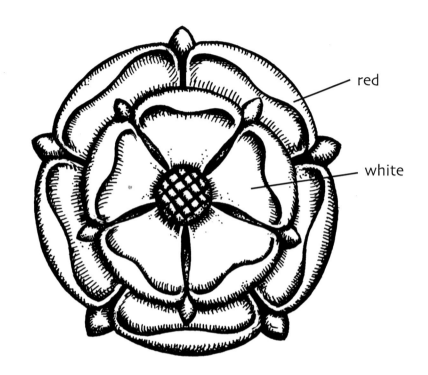

red

white

The Tudor rose

The Tudors

Henry VII	1485–1509
Henry VIII	1509–1547
Edward VI	1547–1553
Mary I	1553–1558
Elizabeth I	1558–1603

The Tudor family

Individual timeline

English history timeline

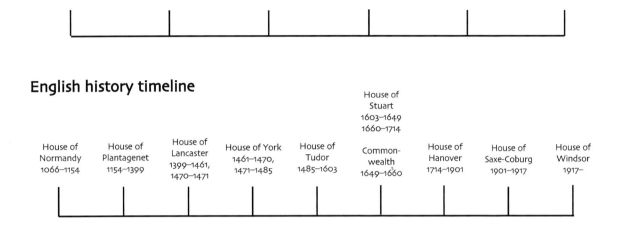

| House of Normandy 1066–1154 | House of Plantagenet 1154–1399 | House of Lancaster 1399–1461, 1470–1471 | House of York 1461–1470, 1471–1485 | House of Tudor 1485–1603 | House of Stuart 1603–1649 1660–1714 / Common-wealth 1649–1660 | House of Hanover 1714–1901 | House of Saxe-Coburg 1901–1917 | House of Windsor 1917– |

Tudor timeline

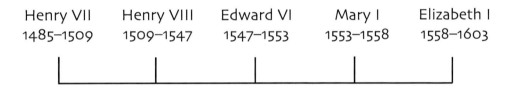

| Henry VII 1485–1509 | Henry VIII 1509–1547 | Edward VI 1547–1553 | Mary I 1553–1558 | Elizabeth I 1558–1603 |

Tudor family tree

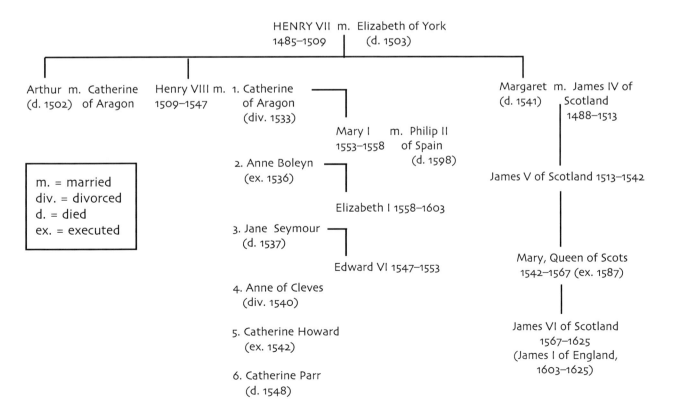

HENRY VII m. Elizabeth of York
1485–1509   (d. 1503)

Arthur m. Catherine
(d. 1502) of Aragon

Henry VIII m.
1509–1547

1. Catherine of Aragon (div. 1533)

Mary I m. Philip II
1553–1558 of Spain
(d. 1598)

2. Anne Boleyn (ex. 1536)

Elizabeth I 1558–1603

3. Jane Seymour (d. 1537)

Edward VI 1547–1553

4. Anne of Cleves (div. 1540)

5. Catherine Howard (ex. 1542)

6. Catherine Parr (d. 1548)

Margaret m. James IV of
(d. 1541)   Scotland
1488–1513

James V of Scotland 1513–1542

Mary, Queen of Scots
1542–1567 (ex. 1587)

James VI of Scotland
1567–1625
(James I of England,
1603–1625)

m. = married
div. = divorced
d. = died
ex. = executed

Name

The Tudor family

Cut out the pictures and the timeline. Stick the timeline onto a clean sheet of paper and stick the labelled pictures in the correct places on the timeline.

Henry VII (1485–1509)

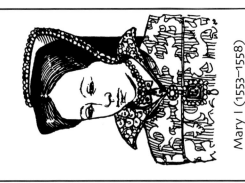

Henry VIII (1509–1547)

Edward VI (1547–1553)

Mary I (1553–1558)

Elizabeth I (1558–1603)

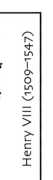

1485   1509   1547   1553   1558   1603

Name _____

The Tudor family

Cut out the timeline and stick it on a clean sheet of paper. Cut out the pictures and name labels, then stick them in the correct places on the timeline.

| Henry VII | Mary I | Henry VIII | Edward VI | Elizabeth I |

1603 — 1558 — 1553 — 1547 — 1509 — 1485

Name

The Tudor family

Cut out the timeline and stick it on a clean sheet of paper. Cut out the pictures and name labels, then stick them on the timeline in the correct order. Draw and name the missing monarch. Add the dates to the timeline.

Henry VII

Mary I

Henry VIII

Edward VI

CURRICULUM FOCUS • TUDORS

Henry VIII

CHAPTER 2

TEACHERS' NOTES

The character of Henry VIII

Henry VIII is best known for his great physical size, yet for many of his younger years he was a very fit, well-trained knight, able to hold his own in jousting tournaments. His spirituality, creativity and indeed his gentleness are all overshadowed by his many marriages and his ruthless attacks on the monasteries (to get his hands on their wealth).

Henry is always painted wearing fashionable clothes, covered in furs and jewels to show his wealth and power. Even his suit of armour (on display in the Tower of London) gives a sense of majestic presence and strength of character not obvious in other monarchs.

Henry's youth

Henry VIII was the second son of Henry VII and Elizabeth of York. He was born at Greenwich Palace on 28 June 1491. Henry was a fine, sturdy boy and his father made sure that he received a thorough training in French and Latin. Henry also became interested in music and theology. He was to grow into a talented and accomplished young man.

When Henry came to the throne in 1509 at the age of 18, he was the most handsome royal figure in Europe, almost six feet tall and of athletic build. Henry was, in fact, an acclaimed sportsman of his day and excelled as a horseman, jouster, huntsman, wrestler and player of real tennis. He loved music and, as well as being a skilled dancer, could sing and play the lute (a type of guitar) and the virginals (a keyboard instrument). As a composer, he is credited with having written the well-known song *Greensleeves*. Henry was also a devout Christian. But above all, he seemed well equipped for kingship and was a young man with a fortune in his hands.

Henry's wars

Henry soon found ways of spending his inheritance, much of it on war. England's traditional enemies were France and Scotland, France's ally. England's ally at the start of Henry's reign was Spain, because the Spanish King Ferdinand was father of Henry's wife, Catherine.

On 16 August 1513, the English and French armies met in battle in France. The English, led by Henry, won this 'Battle of the Spurs' easily; it was so called because of the speed with which the French are said to have fled the field, only their spurs being seen in the distance. Three weeks later, Henry received news that another battle had been won by an English army, at home against Scotland. At the Battle of Flodden on 9 September 1513, the Scottish King James IV (Henry's brother-in-law) and more than 10,000 of his army were killed. A month later, Henry returned in triumph to Dover.

In 1515, Francis I became king of France. In 1520, Henry and Francis met near Calais for a two-week tournament. This lavish event became known as the 'Field of the Cloth of Gold'. Over 5,000 courtiers and hundreds of tents and pavilions were transported across the Channel for the jousting and feasting. But this show of friendship was only on the surface and no treaty resulted.

The 'King's Great Matter'

In the late 1520s, Henry's desire for a male heir, his love for Anne Boleyn and his wish to be divorced from Catherine of Aragon (see Chapter 3) brought him into conflict with the Catholic Church. When the Pope failed to agree to the divorce, Henry took the English Church out of the Pope's control and set himself up as 'Head of the Church in England'. He then appointed Thomas Cranmer as Archbishop of Canterbury, who duly granted the divorce.

Henry attacked the Pope's remaining power base in England, the monasteries. By 1539, nearly 825 monasteries had been closed and all of their wealth went to the king, who became the richest monarch in English history up to that time. Everything was sold – gold and silver plate, ornaments and statues, as well as the buildings and land.

The Pilgrimage of Grace

Not everyone agreed with what Henry was doing. In the north of England, thousands of people began to march towards London to ask Henry to leave the monasteries alone. This was the Pilgrimage of Grace, led by Robert Aske. Henry tricked the protestors into ending their revolt by promising to pardon them, and to look into their complaints. He broke his promise and Aske was hung in chains from a church tower and left to starve to death. This was a warning to everyone that it was unwise to disagree with Henry.

A succession of marriages

Meanwhile, Henry's marriage problems continued. Following Anne Boleyn's execution in 1536, he married Jane Seymour, who died shortly after giving birth to the much longed-for son, Prince Edward. Anne of Cleves was swiftly divorced in 1540 and Catherine Howard executed in 1542. Catherine Parr managed to survive him.

The King's last years

The king's last years were spent in wars with Scotland and France. In 1542, the Scots were defeated at Solway Moss in one of the cheapest battles in history – the English lost seven men and the Scots 20. The Scottish king, James V, died soon after, leaving the throne to his baby daughter, Mary, Queen of Scots. Henry proposed that Mary should be married to his own son, Edward. This idea was rejected and Mary married the king of France.

In 1545, Henry returned from a campaign in France, worried that there would be a French invasion of England. The king stationed himself bravely at Southsea, near Portsmouth, where a French landing was expected. In fact, the matter was decided by a confused sea battle, during which Henry's favourite warship, the *Mary Rose*, keeled over and sank on 29 July 1545. Of the 700 men on board, very few escaped. It was a shocking tragedy for the king as the *Mary Rose* had been to him 'the flower of all the ships that ever sailed'.

Henry was by now well over 50, which was a fair age for Tudor times. He was also a very sick man, with his legs covered in huge ulcers which would not heal and made walking difficult. He had also grown enormously fat – creating a figure that many people remember today. In constant pain, he became more and more irritable. Nursed by his final wife, Catherine Parr, Henry died, aged 55, at Westminster, on the morning of 28 January 1547. On his deathbed, he directed that he was to be buried alongside his favourite wife, Jane Seymour, in St George's Chapel, Windsor. His will named his children, Edward, Mary and Elizabeth, as his successors and they all in turn followed him on the throne. When Prince Edward was told that his father was dead, he clung crying to Princess Elizabeth. Great, terrifying Henry had been replaced by a nine-year-old boy.

Important dates in Henry's life

1491   Henry VIII born, second son of Henry VII and Elizabeth of York.

1501   Henry becomes heir to the throne of England when his older brother, Arthur, dies.

1509   On the death of Henry VII, Henry VIII becomes king of England and marries Catherine of Aragon.

1511   Henry's favourite warship, the *Mary Rose*, is launched.

1515   Henry's great rival, Francis I, becomes king of France.

1516   Catherine of Aragon gives birth to Princess Mary.

1520   Henry VIII meets Francis I at the Field of the Cloth of Gold.

1527   Henry's request to the Pope for a divorce is refused.

1529   Cardinal Wolsey, Henry's chief minister, fails to persuade the Pope to grant Henry a divorce, falls from favour, and then dies.

1533   Henry divorces Catherine of Aragon, without the Pope's permission, and marries Anne Boleyn. Anne gives birth to Princess Elizabeth.

1534   Henry replaces the Pope as head of the English Church.

1536   Anne Boleyn is executed. Henry marries Jane Seymour.

1537   Jane Seymour gives birth to a son, Edward, but dies 12 days later.

1539   Over 800 monasteries had been closed and their wealth taken by Henry.

1540   Henry marries Anne of Cleves and divorces her. Cromwell is beheaded for arranging the marriage. Henry marries Catherine Howard.

1542   Catherine Howard is beheaded and Henry marries Catherine Parr, his sixth and final wife.

1545   The *Mary Rose* sinks.

1547   Henry VIII dies, aged 55. Francis I dies in the same year.

Henry VIII

LESSON PLAN

History objectives (Unit 7)

- About the appearance and character of Henry VIII.
- What information can be gathered about Henry VIII from portraits and written sources.
- About the power and importance of a Tudor king.
- To identify what monarchs did.

Resources

- Generic sheets 1–3 (pages 19–21)
- Activity sheets 1–3 (pages 22–24)
- A whiteboard or flip chart

Starting points: *whole class*

Choose a current popular figure (such as a pop star or famous footballer) and ask the children to tell you as much as they can about them. Note the information on the board under headings such as appearance, hobbies, talents, wealth and work. Repeat the exercise for today's monarch, challenging the children to recall everything they know about her and her family, using the same headings.

Using the information in the teachers' notes, briefly give some details of Henry VIII's life, highlighting his hobbies, his wealth and his political difficulties with France and Scotland. The key questions for the children to answer are 'What sort of person was this king?' and 'What did he look like?'

Before the lesson, cut out the individual illustrations on Generic sheets 1 and 2. Give the children the pictures of Henry from Generic sheet 1. Ask questions such as:

- What did Henry look like as a boy? Does he look happy? Does he look healthy?
- What did Henry look like as a young man? Do his clothes make him look wealthy? Is he wearing jewels? Why do you think he has a beard?
- What is the difference between Henry as a young man and Henry in middle age? Are his clothes even more spectacular? Why do you think his clothes cover his neck? Do you think he is wearing more jewels to hide the fact that he is becoming less handsome?
- How would you describe Henry's face in his old age? Why do you think it is all puffy? What do

Henry's hands look like? Does Henry look ill? Why do you think Henry is so heavily dressed? What do you think his clothes are hiding?

Ask the children to compare the four portraits. How can they tell that Henry is getting older? How did his clothes change his appearance?

Give the children the pictures from Generic sheet 2. Ask what the pictures can tell us about Henry's lifestyle. Ask questions such as:

- *Real tennis*: At what age do you think Henry played this sport? Did he need to be energetic? Would only rich people have had the time to play real tennis? Why? Could Henry have played tennis in later life? Did he grow too large to play or exercise properly?
- *Lute and virginals*: Henry loved music – how did music help him? Did it help his creative side? Do these look difficult instruments to play?
- *Riding and hunting*: Henry loved riding throughout his life. How do you think the horse would feel to have someone as heavy as Henry on its back? What does the big palace in the picture tell you about Henry's homes?
- *Armour*: This famous armour is on display in the Tower of London. What sort of protection did this give Henry? Do you think the armour shows how big and strong Henry was? Do you think it just shows how well protected he would be in battle? Do you think a person would need to be wealthy to own such armour? Why? Why not?

Give the children Generic sheet 3. Tell them about the Field of the Cloth of Gold: the huge party Henry had with the king of France, with each king trying to outdo the other. Ask:

- What does this tell you about how Henry VIII would be seen by other monarchs? Was his lifestyle so rich that no expense was spared to make him appear all-powerful to his enemies?

Tell the children that they are going to build up a picture of Henry VIII and his lifestyle.

Group activities

Activity sheet 1
This sheet is aimed at children who need more support. The children are asked to choose descriptive words (from a word bank) to describe Henry accurately. They have to decide which of the words describe Henry as a young man, and which as an old man. Then they have to complete sentences using the words.

Activity sheet 2
This sheet is aimed at children who are more independent workers. The children are asked to circle the given words that describe Henry as a young man, and underline the words that describe him as an old man. (Some words belong in both categories.) Then the children have to write two paragraphs about Henry: one about his youth and one about his old age.

Activity sheet 3
This sheet is aimed at more able children. They have to make a list of descriptive words to describe Henry as a young man. Then they repeat this for Henry's old age. They have to make a Venn diagram to show words that apply to both stages of Henry's life. Then they have to write a pen portrait of Henry, including young and old aspects of his character and appearance.

Plenary session

Remind the children of the headings used at the start of the lesson to describe the famous person. Recap on some of the highlights of Henry's life from the teachers' notes. Challenge the children to use the same headings to describe Henry VIII. Ask 'How does someone's appearance change as they get older?', 'Do people try to disguise the fact that they are getting older?' and 'While Henry VIII is remembered for his physical size, what do you think he should be remembered for?'

Ideas for support

If a child has difficulty reading the descriptive words, read them aloud and put them into contextual sentences to help recognition.

The more able children could use dictionaries and a thesaurus to find descriptive words. Aim to keep their Venn diagrams simple.

Ideas for extension

Different children could paint portraits of Henry at different stages of his life. These could be displayed on a frieze. Pictures showing Henry's character and lifestyle could form a second frieze.

The children could make a life-size model of Henry VIII for the centre of the display. (At the end of his life his waist measurement was 147cm and he was 1.88m tall.)

A detailed plan of the 'Field of the Cloth of Gold' could be expressed through art forms such as tapestry, painting or collage.

Find out more about the game of real tennis.

Listen to music of the Tudor period. Try to reproduce the sound on modern instruments.

Linked ICT activities

Using a word processing program, such as *Textease* (see Useful resources on page 118), create word banks for the children to support their writing about different events in Henry's life, such as the sinking of the *Mary Rose* or the names of his wives.

Tell the children that they are going to work in pairs to write a diary for a day describing a significant date in Henry's life. They have to explain what happened in the morning, afternoon and evening of this day as though they were watching the event take place. Give each pair a different event, such as a wedding, the sinking of the *Mary Rose* or an execution. Encourage them to imagine and write about what it would have been like to be at this event and how Henry behaved.

Encourage the children to find information about the event they have been given. They can use CD-Roms, but check with your LEA guidelines on children using search engines before allowing them to search the internet.

Use the completed diaries to display alongside the class timeline of events. Leave copies of the diaries in the school library for other children to read. If your school has a website that contains curriculum content, publish the diaries on the website for others to read.

Henry VIII

Henry as a young boy

Henry as a young man

Henry in middle age

Henry in old age

Henry VIII

Real tennis: one sport played by an energetic Henry.

Lute and virginals: music was a great love of Henry's.

Henry enjoyed riding and hunting for most of his life.

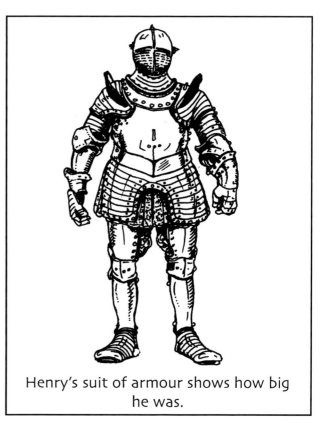

Henry's suit of armour shows how big he was.

PHOTOCOPIABLE

Henry VIII

The Field of the Cloth of Gold

Name _____

Henry VIII

Circle the words that you think describe Henry VIII.

WORD BANK

attractive	flamboyant	impatient	slim	heavy
handsome	sporty	ugly	obese	creative	grumpy
ill	fierce	dignified	clean-shaven	tall	fit
large	short	scruffy	musical	happy

Write the words you have circled into these two columns. Some words will go in both columns.

young Henry	old Henry

Using the word bank, complete these sentences:

When Henry VIII was a young man, he was h _ _ _ _ _ _ _ _ , h _ _ _ _ _
and s _ _ _ . He was f _ _ , s _ _ _ _ _ _ and m _ _ _ _ _ _ _ .

When Henry VIII was an old man, he was h _ _ _ _ _ , g _ _ _ _ _ _ and
u _ _ _ . He was still m _ _ _ _ _ _ _ , but not very s _ _ _ _ _ _ .

Name _____

Henry VIII

Circle the words in the word bank that you think accurately describe
Henry VIII as a young man.

WORD BANK

attractive	flamboyant	impatient	slim	heavy
handsome	sporty	ugly	obese	creative	grumpy
ill	fierce	dignified	clean-shaven	tall	fit
large	short	scruffy	musical	happy

Underline the words in the word bank that you think accurately describe
Henry VIII as an old man. Some words may already be circled.

Using the words you have circled, write a paragraph about Henry as a young man.

Using the words you have underlined and some you have circled, write a paragraph
about Henry as an old man.

Name _____

Henry VIII

Add your own descriptive words to the list below to describe Henry
as a young man:

fun loving

sporty

fashionable

handsome

flamboyant

Add your own descriptive words to the list below to describe Henry as an old man:

heavy

tired

heavily clothed

sad

Which descriptive words apply to Henry when he was young as well as
when he was old?

On the back of this sheet, use both your lists to draw a Venn diagram to show
words that apply to Henry as:
- a young man
- an old man
- both a young man and an old man.

Using this information, create a pen portrait of Henry, covering both young and
old aspects of his character and his appearance.

Henry VIII's six wives

CHAPTER 3

TEACHERS' NOTES

Royal marriages

Henry's many marriages began in the normal way for royal children of his day. He was engaged to be married, while still a boy, to a girl-princess. The arrangements were made by the parents of both families and the main purpose of the marriage was political.

Catherine of Aragon

Catherine of Aragon was born on 16 December 1485, daughter of Ferdinand and Isabella of Spain. By 1489, she was engaged to be married to Henry VII's first son, Arthur, the main aim being to unite the thrones of England and Spain. Many years passed before the marriage could take place, but at last in 1501, shortly before her sixteenth birthday, Catherine was married to the 14-year-old Arthur.

Yet within six months, Arthur was dead. To maintain the Anglo-Spanish alliance, Catherine then became betrothed to Arthur's younger brother. Henry was only 11 and too young to marry for at least two years. However, although Catherine remained in England, Anglo-Spanish relations deteriorated and the couple were not married until after Henry had ascended the throne in 1509. A papal bull of dispensation was obtained from Pope Julius II in order to overcome the obstacle that Catherine had previously been married to Arthur.

Contemporary accounts show that Henry was greatly attracted to his wife and that the marriage started off as a happy one. Catherine was an intelligent, accomplished and suitable companion for a young and active king. However, the main duty of a queen was to provide male heirs to the throne in order to ensure an undisputed succession on the king's death. Although Catherine gave birth to six children, only one survived – Princess Mary, born in 1516.

Henry was becoming increasingly unhappy and, by 1527 when the 42-year-old queen was past child-bearing age, he started to look at ways of dissolving the marriage in order that he could marry again. This action, known as the 'King's Great Matter',

revolved around a passage Henry found in the Bible from Leviticus 20: 21 stating that 'If a man shall take his brother's wife it is an unclean thing ... they shall be childless.' Henry and Catherine were not childless, but a daughter was of no use to the king's succession. Henry felt that God was punishing him for marrying his brother's widow and that this punishment was to deny him a son.

Finally, in 1533, Henry overruled the authority of the Pope, who had refused to cooperate in divorce proceedings, and arranged for Thomas Cranmer, Archbishop of Canterbury, to annul the marriage.

Catherine was then given the title of Princess Dowager of Wales, which showed that she had been Arthur's widow, but had never been Henry's wife. She lived for three more years, banished from court and separated from her daughter, Mary. She died at Kimbolton on 7 January 1536, aged 50. She was buried in Peterborough Abbey. Henry did not attend the funeral.

Anne Boleyn

Anne Boleyn was the daughter of a London merchant, Thomas Boleyn, who had married into the noble Howard family. Through her mother, Anne was a niece of the Duke of Norfolk. Little is known for certain about her early years, but Anne was probably born in 1502 at Hever in Kent.

Soon after the marriage of Anne's sister Mary to Louis XII of France in 1514, Anne was sent to the French court for her education and she remained there for eight years. On her return to England, she came to Henry VIII's court and, although she did not make an immediate impression on the king, she seems to have attracted the attention of other men and was about to become engaged to Henry Percy. Cardinal Wolsey (perhaps acting for the king) stepped in to prevent this liaison. Anne despised Wolsey for this act and never forgave him.

Anne's sister, Mary, was Henry's mistress until the king fell in love with Anne in about 1525. However, Anne refused to give in to the king's advances until he promised to marry her. By about 1530, Henry's relationship with Anne was being talked about openly, and in the following year Catherine was banished from court. At some time either towards the end of 1532 or the beginning of 1533, Henry secretly married Anne Boleyn. He still stuck vehemently to the belief that he and Catherine had never been legally married and this was backed up on 23 May 1533 when Archbishop Cranmer pronounced the marriage between Henry and Catherine invalid.

On 7 September, Anne gave birth to a girl, Elizabeth. Henry made little attempt to conceal his disappointment and when in January 1536 she lost a son in childbirth, Anne finally lost the king's favour. Henry even accused Anne's brother and four other courtiers of not only being intimate with her, but also plotting to assassinate him. They were arrested and executed. Anne was accused of treason and beheaded by a French swordsman on 19 May 1536. Henry also dissolved their marriage shortly before the execution. Anne's body was buried in the Tower of London.

Jane Seymour

Jane Seymour, daughter of Sir John Seymour, served as a lady-in-waiting to both Catherine of Aragon and Anne Boleyn. She may have attracted the king's attention when he visited her father at his home of Wolf Hall in 1535, but we hear no mention of any affair until February 1536, when courtiers began to talk about the possibility of Jane becoming queen. The affair was kept quiet until Anne Boleyn was beheaded in May 1536, but then a day after her execution Jane was engaged to Henry and they were married ten days later.

On 12 October 1537, in the twenty-ninth year of Henry's reign, Jane bore him the son he so desperately wanted. Prince Edward was born at Hampton Court and three days later was christened. Princess Mary, now in favour with her father, was godmother, and Queen Jane, although very weak, was present.

Unfortunately, Jane never fully recovered from the birth and died on 24 October 1537. She was buried in the tomb that Henry was preparing for himself at Windsor, and is the only one of his wives to share his grave.

Anne of Cleves

Anne of Cleves, sister of the German Duke of Cleves, married Henry on 6 January 1540. The marriage was arranged to make an alliance with the German Protestant rulers, but Henry also insisted that his future bride should be pleasant to look at. He therefore had his court painter, Holbein, paint her likeness before the marriage was agreed. But even though Henry approved of her painting and went ahead with the marriage after having seen her in real life, he claimed to find her 'physically repulsive', referring to her as the Flanders' Mare. He had the marriage dissolved on the grounds of non-consummation. Anne also disliked two of Henry's passions – books and music – and this did not help her relationship with the king.

Anne herself was cooperative throughout the divorce proceedings. She was given the title of King's Sister and a large income for life, provided she remain in England. She happily agreed and went on to live until 1557.

Catherine Howard

Catherine Howard was the daughter of Lord Edmund Howard and a first cousin of Anne Boleyn. She served as a maid of honour to Anne of Cleves, and was married to Henry VIII on 28 July 1540, 16 days after his divorce from Anne of Cleves. Henry was by now nearly 50, whereas Catherine was only a teenager, yet for 14 months the marriage was a great success. Henry recovered much of his former enjoyment of life, and hunting, feasting and dancing returned to court.

But in November 1541, evidence that Catherine had previously had affairs was presented to the king. Henry was initially dumbstruck, but when he was told that Catherine had also been flirting behind his back, and her secretary, Francis Dereham, was named, he asked for further investigations.

This proved to be her downfall and there could be no mercy. She went the same way as her cousin Anne Boleyn. She was tried and condemned, and on 13 February 1542 she was beheaded at the Tower of London.

Catherine Parr

Catherine Parr was the daughter of Sir Thomas Parr of Kendall, a country squire. At the time of her marriage to Henry VIII on 12 July 1543, Catherine was 31 years old and had previously been widowed twice. When she married Henry, she became as much a nurse to him as a wife. She knew how to make him laugh and ease the pain of old age. She was an intelligent woman who could speak Latin, Greek and French. She even managed to become friends with Henry's three children, Mary, Elizabeth and Edward, who were all encouraged in their studies.

Catherine outlived the king, who died in January 1547, and in fact married for a fourth time. Thomas Seymour was the brother of Jane and uncle of Prince Edward, and Catherine had been in love with him before her marriage to Henry. She now was free to marry Thomas and on 30 August 1548 gave birth to his child. She died soon after on 7 September and was buried at the Seymour manor of Sudeley (Gloucestershire).

LESSON PLAN

Henry VIII's six wives

History objectives (Unit 7)
- The names and order of Henry VIII's wives.
- To extract information from portraits and descriptions.

Resources

- Generic sheets 1 and 2 (pages 30 and 31)
- Activity sheets 1–3 (pages 32–34)

Starting points: *whole class*

Ask the children to draw a portrait of a friend. Invite them to guess who each of the portraits portrays. How can they tell? Then ask them to draw a portrait of someone in their family, adding a hat or hairstyle that will help others to recognise whether the person is young or old, male or female.

Hand out copies of the pictures of Henry's six wives on Generic sheet 1. Ask the children to describe some of the women's basic facial features. How are the women different from one another?

Using the details from the teachers' notes, give the children some facts about each of the women. Hand out copies of Generic sheet 2 for their reference. Talk about the differences between the lives and personalities of the six wives.

Invite a volunteer to the front of the class. Show them the name of one of Henry's wives, making sure that the other children do not see. Then invite them to describe the secret wife or, if confident enough, pretend to be that wife (for example, 'I am Henry's fifth wife…'). The class then have to decide which wife is being described, using the pictures and text on Generic sheets 1 and 2 if necessary.

Cut out the words and pictures from the two sheets and put them together, with each wife on a different sheet. This could also be done on an OHP.

Tell the children that they are now going to complete a chart and a wordsearch about Henry's wives. (The answers are on page 114.)

Group activities

Activity sheet 1

This sheet is aimed at children who need more support. They have to complete the chart with information about each of Henry's six wives. Two have been done for them as examples. They are then asked to complete some clues with the words provided, then find these words in the wordsearch.

Activity sheet 2

This sheet is aimed at children who can work independently. They have to fill in the chart with information about each of Henry's six wives. They are then asked to complete some clues and then find the words in the wordsearch.

Activity sheet 3

This sheet is aimed at more able children. They have to create a chart with information about each of Henry's six wives. They are then asked to write the clues for a wordsearch.

Plenary session

Look again at the pictures of Henry's wives (Generic sheet 1). Ask the children which wife they would have liked to have been and why. Then ask them to pretend to be Henry VIII and try to work out which wife they think would be his favourite and why. Ask them to write the numbers 1 to 6. Then call out the wives' names one by one, which they have to write next to the correct numbers.

Ideas for support

For children who find it difficult to transfer information from a list of facts to a chart, help them fill in one row or one column at a time. Use the information from Generic sheet 2. It might help to cut up Generic sheet 2 into six sections (one for each wife), so that the children do not have to look at so much information at once.

For children working independently on the chart, give clues such as 'Fill in all the years of birth first'.

Children who are creating their own clues to the wordsearch can be guided towards the information on Generic sheet 2 or to other sources such as the National Portrait Gallery website (see Useful resources on page 117).

Ideas for extension

Arrange a visit to the National Portrait Gallery (or go to the website) for the children to make sketches in preparation for painting their own portraits of Henry's wives. (See Useful resources on page 117.) They could use a variety of art materials from collage to crayon to create their final portrait. Pottery busts could also be made.

Invite the children to imagine what it would be like to be a wife of Henry VIII. Think about the feelings of the different women – excited at being chosen, disappointed at not being liked any more or fear for their children. It would also be interesting for the children to imagine themselves as Henry VIII, wanting a son so badly, and his different reactions to his different wives. Once these ideas have been explored, a small play could be put together to illustrate Henry's complicated life.

Challenge the children to use information sources to find out as much as they can about one or more of Henry's wives. They could then write a diary entry pretending to be one of the wives. What might they write about life with Henry?

Linked ICT activities

Using illustrations and images from the internet and other resources, look at the way in which Henry and his wives would have posed to have their portraits painted. Talk to the children about how we keep pictures of ourselves today. Discuss the differences between painting a portrait and taking a photograph (the expense, the time, the materials). Compare how we record events with images today, using photographs, video and sound, with how events would have been recorded in the past using portraits, pictures and written diaries.

Using a child-friendly digital camera (see Useful resources on page 119) or a still camera, tell the children that they are going to create their own class modern portrait gallery. Collect a set of props and disguises for them to use for their portrait. Tell them that they are going to create a disguise for their portrait and become a fictitious king or queen. Provide a colourful backdrop for the portrait and mount the final photograph on some patterned wrapping paper to give a modern look to the image.

The finished class portrait gallery could then be used by the children as a starting point for literacy activities. Ask the children to choose a character from the gallery and, using a word processing program, write a brief description of the character and what they are famous for. If the portraits are digital, they can be included with the description.

Henry VIII's six wives

Catherine of Aragon

Anne Boleyn

Jane Seymour

Anne of Cleves

Catherine Howard

Catherine Parr

Henry VIII's six wives

The six wives of Henry VIII

Henry married three Catherines, two Annes and one Jane.
Here are some facts about each wife.

Catherine of Aragon
- Born 1485.
- Daughter of Ferdinand and Isabella of Spain.
- First married to Prince Arthur, eldest son of Henry VII.
- Married Henry VIII in June 1509.
- Had several children, but only one survived – a daughter, Princess Mary.
- Henry divorced Catherine in June 1533.
- Died in 1536, aged 50.

Anne Boleyn
- Born 1502.
- Second wife of Henry VIII.
- Married Henry in January 1533.
- Had a daughter, Elizabeth, but not the son Henry longed for.
- Henry grew tired of Anne, charged her with treason and had her beheaded in the Tower of London on 19 May 1536.
- She was known as 'Anne of a Thousand Days'.

Jane Seymour
- Born 1509.
- Third and favourite wife of Henry VIII.
- Married Henry in May/June 1536.
- Had one child, Prince Edward, born 12 October 1537.
- Died on 24 October 1537.
- Buried in the tomb Henry was preparing for himself at Windsor Castle.

Anne of Cleves
- Born 1515.
- Fourth wife of Henry VIII.
- Anne was a German princess and married in January 1540 for political reasons.
- Henry had only seen a portrait of Anne, and when she arrived in England he found her dull and unattractive.
- Divorced in July 1540.
- Anne spoke no English and had no children.
- Died in 1557.
- Known as the 'Flanders' Mare'.

Catherine Howard
- Born 1521.
- Fifth wife of Henry VIII.
- Married in July 1540; she was 30 years younger than her husband.
- Had no children.
- Catherine was the cousin of Anne Boleyn and her life ended in the same way – she was beheaded in February 1542 for treason.

Catherine Parr
- Born 1512.
- Sixth and final wife of Henry VIII.
- Married in July 1543 by which time Henry was quite ill, so Catherine spent most of her time nursing him.
- Had no children with Henry.
- After the king's death in 1547, she married Thomas Seymour and died in 1548.

Name _____

Henry VIII's six wives

Complete this grid. Use the descriptions and pictures of Henry VIII's six wives to help you. Two examples have been done for you.

Henry VIII's wives	Year of birth	Date of marriage	How long queen	Name of child	Date of death	One fact about her
Catherine of Aragon	1485	1509	24 years	Mary	1536	Henry divorced her
Anne Boleyn						
Jane Seymour						
Anne of Cleves	1515	1540	6 months	_	1557	spoke no English
Catherine Howard						
Catherine Parr						

Complete the clues and find the answers in the wordsearch.
Use the word box to help you.

s	a	p	a	r	r	b
e	s	e	v	e	l	c
y	h	o	w	a	r	d
m	c	g	n	h	e	i
o	j	n	l	q	o	s
u	e	m	a	r	y	r
r	m	f	p	n	d	k

WORD BOX
Parr   Seymour   Anne
Mary   Howard   Cleves

1. Henry VIII's favourite wife was Jane S_____
2. Anne of C_____ came from Germany.
3. Henry VIII's last wife was Catherine P_____
4. Catherine H_____ was beheaded.
5. Catherine of Aragon had a daughter called M_____
6. Two of Henry VIII's wives were called A_____

Name _____

Henry VIII's six wives

Draw up a larger copy of this grid. Complete the grid. Use the descriptions and pictures about Henry VIII's six wives to help you.

Henry VIII's wives	Year of birth	Date of marriage	How long queen	Name of child	Date of death	One fact about her
Catherine of Aragon						
Anne Boleyn						
Jane Seymour						
Anne of Cleves						
Catherine Howard						
Catherine Parr						

Complete the clues and find the answers in the wordsearch.

s	a	p	a	r	r	b
e	s	e	v	e	l	c
y	h	o	w	a	r	d
m	c	g	n	h	e	i
o	j	n	l	q	o	s
u	e	m	a	r	y	r
r	m	f	p	n	d	k

1. Henry VIII's favourite wife was Jane S_____
2. Anne of C_____ came from Germany.
3. Henry VIII's last wife was Catherine P_____
4. Catherine H_____ was beheaded.
5. Catherine of Aragon had a daughter called M_____
6. Two of Henry VIII's wives were called A_____

Henry VIII's six wives

On the back of this sheet, draw up a large chart.
Use these column headings:

- Henry VIII's wives
- Year of birth
- Date of marriage
- How long queen
- Name of child
- Date of death
- One fact about her

Write the names of Henry's wives in column 1.
Complete the grid. Use the descriptions and pictures of Henry VIII to help you.

Make up clues for this wordsearch.
All the answers are the names of Henry VIII's wives or children.

s	a	p	a	r	r	b
e	s	e	v	e	l	c
y	h	o	w	a	r	d
m	c	g	n	h	e	i
o	j	n	l	q	o	s
u	e	m	a	r	y	r
r	m	f	p	n	d	k

CLUES

1.

2.

3.

4.

5.

6.

Henry VIII's marriages

CHAPTER 4

TEACHERS' NOTES

Marriage in Tudor times

In Tudor times, whether a father was rich or poor, he was head of the household and expected to rule his family as a king ruled his subjects. This meant that he often arranged marriages for his children. Poor people tended to get married later than rich people as they usually could not afford to do so until they reached their mid-twenties. Children were encouraged to marry into families that were as well off or better off than their own. Parents often said that if their children married someone they disapproved of, they would leave them nothing in their wills.

Tudor weddings

Tudor weddings were colourful events, full of music and noise. The bride and groom married in church and, if the couple were poor, a collection was often made to give them a good start to their married life.

Most married women would not find life easy. The Church taught that a woman's main role in life was to bear children. Women could expect to become pregnant in nearly every year of their lives until they became too old to have children. Giving birth was dangerous for the mother and being born was dangerous for the baby. Because many babies died within days of birth, they were baptised at once. Despite the many hardships, most girls probably did want to get married, as in Tudor times there were no careers for women. A girl's only other future would be to stay at home with her parents and spend her time spinning. This is why unmarried women were called spinsters.

When a girl did get married it was for life. Nowadays divorce is common, but in sixteenth-century England it was a rare occurrence. The reason for this was that the Pope, the head of the Catholic Church, controlled the Church in England and granted divorce only in exceptional circumstances.

Henry VIII's marriages

Although Henry VIII married six times, he spent almost half his life with his first wife, Catherine of Aragon. The rot set in when he divorced her in 1533, and the following ten years saw him going through the wedding ceremony with another five women.

Henry came to the throne in April 1509 and less than two months later married his brother Arthur's widow, Catherine. Arthur and Catherine's marriage was a political alliance to ensure peace with Spain, and had been arranged by Henry's father, Henry VII, and Catherine's father, Ferdinand of Spain, when Arthur, Henry and Catherine were still children. The Spanish king and queen also paid Henry VII a dowry when the engagement took place.

Henry and Catherine's first child was stillborn the following year, but on New Year's Day 1511 a son was born, and Henry organised a royal tournament to celebrate the birth of a prince. The baby died ten days later. In spite of Catherine being pregnant several times over the next ten years, only one child, Mary, born in 1516, lived. Catherine became pregnant for the last time in 1518. Henry was desperate for a male heir, yet continued to remain a devoted husband for many years to come. He did have affairs with other women, one being Elizabeth Blount, who bore him a son called Henry Fitzroy, but this was not unknown for kings of England.

The problem of an heir

In Tudor times a king would lead his armies into battle, forge alliances and bring honour to his kingdom. Henry wanted a male heir to carry on where he left off. History was to prove that a queen could be just as successful.

In 1527, the 'King's Great Matter' was being talked about at court. Catherine was now 42 and past her childbearing years. Henry meanwhile was still only 36 and at his physical peak. The king saw that the only way to get a male heir was to divorce Catherine. He even had a replacement in mind – Anne Boleyn. Even though the Catholic Church was anti-divorce, Henry could see no problem in being granted one, as firstly he was a king and secondly he also knew that there was a passage in the Bible which said that a man should not marry his brother's widow, which is what he had done (see Chapter 3). In fact, the Pope had granted special permission to allow Henry to marry Catherine. Surely this permission could just be cancelled!

However, Catherine was the aunt of Charles V, the Holy Roman Emperor, and the current pope, Clement VII, had been a prisoner of Charles. He would have been in great trouble if he had agreed to Henry's demand to end the marriage. Matters were finally resolved in 1532 when Henry, with the help of his Chancellor, Thomas Cromwell, saw that the only way to get his divorce was to break from the Pope completely and declare himself Head of the Church in England. He then married Anne and persuaded Archbishop Cranmer to declare his marriage to Catherine null and void. Catherine was banished from court and died three years later in 1536.

Anne gave birth to a baby girl, Elizabeth, in September 1533, but still no legitimate male heir appeared. Henry was so angered by this that he stayed away from Elizabeth's christening. Anne's two other pregnancies ended in miscarriages. Less than three years after their marriage, Henry accused Anne of being unfaithful and had her executed on 19 May 1536.

The quest continues

Henry's quest for a male heir had not been a success. By this time, he was on poor terms with the Pope and badly needed the support of his nobles, especially those followers of the new Protestant faith. Wife number three, therefore, was the daughter of one of the most powerful families in the country. Jane Seymour was reputedly Henry's favourite wife. In October 1537, much to Henry's joy and delight, she gave birth to the longed for son, who was named Edward. Tragically, Jane died days later, her death hardly noticed amidst the rejoicing that England at last had a male heir. But Henry was sad to see her die and did not marry again for three years.

Charles V, Holy Roman Emperor of the vast Habsburg Empire and king of Spain, had

condemned Protestantism and Henry was keen to gain the support of a Protestant country to counter any hostility against him. In 1540 he married a German princess, Anne of Cleves. The marriage was to be a disaster. It was settled without Henry having actually met Anne, the king relying instead on a portrait painted by the court artist, Holbein.

Henry liked the portrait, but not the ugly, clumsy and not over-clean 'real life' Anne. She supposedly even smelled of the garlic that she liked to chew. The king was heard to have said that he had married a 'Flanders' Mare'. They never lived together as husband and wife and Henry divorced Anne six months after their marriage. Thomas Cromwell, Henry's chief minister, was executed for suggesting Anne as a suitable bride. This alliance had not worked.

By now the political climate in England had changed a little, so the king needed to please the English Catholics. A month after his last divorce, Henry married Catherine Howard, niece of the Catholic Duke of Norfolk and cousin of Anne Boleyn. Although they had 14 months of very happy marriage, evidence was presented to Henry that Catherine was being unfaithful to him and he had her tried, condemned and executed.

The final years

Catherine Parr was Henry's last wife and acted more as a nurse to him in his old age. She had been widowed twice before and was a good companion for him in his last years. Having survived accusations of unfaithfulness and religious beliefs that went against the king's own beliefs, Catherine was still with Henry when he died in 1547. She was the only wife to outlive him.

Henry had married six times, first and foremost to gain a legitimate male heir, secondly for political reasons, both home and abroad, and thirdly for companionship. It seems strange that his most contented marriage was probably his last.

Henry VIII's marriages

LESSON PLAN

History objectives (Unit 7)
- About the reasons for royal marriages.
- That building alliances through marriage was important in the Tudor period.
- About the reasons for Henry's divorce from Catherine of Aragon.
- About the reasons for and results of Henry's marriages to Anne Boleyn and Jane Seymour.

Resources

- Generic sheets 1 and 2 (pages 39 and 40)
- Activity sheets 1–3 (pages 41–43)

Starting points: *whole class*

Open a class discussion with the question 'Why do you come to school?' Prompt answers if necessary to include reasons such as:

- 'I want to learn.'
- 'I want to be with my friends.'
- 'My parents say I have to come.'
- 'The government says I have to go to school until I am 16.'

Explain to the children that these are all reasons for coming to school and that there are often many different reasons for doing the same thing. Parents have a different outlook from children, teachers and the government. So when we look back in history, we have to look at the reasons why things happened. Display the question 'Why?' in the centre of the board to prompt the children's thinking for this lesson.

Tell the children they are going to find out why Henry VIII married so many times. Show them the table of the four main reasons for Henry's marriages on Generic sheet 1.

- To make alliances to strengthen England's relations with other countries. Ask where Catherine of Aragon came from (Spain), and Anne of Cleves (Germany). Ask 'Why did England need to be friendly with these countries?' (To help fight against common enemies such as France.)
- Falling in love. Henry is said to have loved Anne Boleyn, Jane Seymour, Catherine Howard and Catherine Parr.

- The need for Henry to have power in England over the Church. He married Jane Seymour to gain Protestant support, and Catherine Howard to gain Catholic support. Both women belonged to wealthy, influential families.
- The need for a male heir. Henry wanted a son to carry on the Tudor name. Kings also led their armies in battle.

Then show the children the table on Generic sheet 2. Discuss each of the four reasons why Henry married six times and the consequences of his actions on the six women involved. Encourage the children to imagine how the women must have felt.

Tell the children that they are now going to do an activity to show why Henry married his wives. (The answers are on page 114.)

Group activities

Activity sheet 1
This sheet is aimed at children who need more support. They have a column of pictures of Henry's wives (in chronological order) on the left of the sheet. On the right they have a jumbled list of reasons why Henry married them. They have to link the reasons to the wives. Some reasons apply to more than one wife. One example is given. Then they have to write in their own words why Henry married six times.

Activity sheet 2
This sheet is aimed at children who can work independently. They have to match six sentence-starters to six sentence endings to make correct statements about Henry's wives. Next they have to write the statements in chronological order. Then they have to write in their own words why Henry married six times.

Activity sheet 3

This sheet is aimed at more able children. The children have to write their own sentences for each wife, to say why Henry married her. They may use other information sources to help.

Plenary session

Look at the question 'Why?' again. Ask the children if they can think of some 'why' questions about Henry VIII. Choose two or three questions that they have offered and invite oral answers. Finally, look again at the complicated life of Henry VIII and finish with the thought that although we can try to guess at the reasons why things happened in history we can never be sure whether we are right or wrong. However, everyone's opinion is of value.

Ideas for support

To help children who find it difficult to understand that there are different reasons for doing things, start with the reason 'falling in love'. Guide them to Anne Boleyn, because Henry fell in love with her first. Ask 'Do you think Henry loved his other wives?' and listen to their reasons. (The only wife Henry didn't like was Anne of Cleves, so children's opinions on this subjective answer can be correct.)

When looking at foreign alliances, emphasise the friendship with other countries (Spain at the start of his reign because of their common enemy, France). Alliances for religious reasons are not easy to understand, but Generic sheet 2 may be helpful.

Ideas for extension

Look at other aspects of Tudor life and try to work out reasons why things happened as they did – for example, why do we remember Henry VIII as being so large? Why does everyone know Henry VIII had six wives? Did any other monarch have more than one wife?

More able children could explore the concept of the power of a monarch over their subjects, looking at Tudor monarchs through independent research.

Linked ICT activities

Discuss with the children what happens today before a wedding takes place. How do people formally ask you to go to a wedding? Discuss why we send invitations and what an invitation tells us. Ask them to bring in any invitations they may have at home (provided they have permission from their parents/carers). Show some examples of wedding and other invitations. Tell the children that these invitations will probably have been produced using a computer graphics program for the images and a word processing program for the text.

Ask them to imagine what a Tudor wedding may have been like. What might the wedding invitations look like? (Ink on parchment or vellum rolled into a scroll or folded.)

Tell the children that they are going to create a wedding invitation for one of Henry VIII's weddings.

Using a graphics program such as *Dazzle* or Microsoft *Paintbrush* (see Useful resources on page 118), show the children how to insert a clip art picture onto their page. Using the invitations brought in from home for ideas, show them how to add some text to the picture to create the design.

Discuss with the children what they would need to include on the invitation to let people know when and where the wedding will take place. Show them how to include this text on their invitation page.

Henry VIII's marriages

Reasons why Henry VIII married six times

Need for alliances abroad	Falling in love	Need for power in England through alliances	Need for a male heir
Catherine of Aragon (with Spain against France)	Anne Boleyn	Jane Seymour (with the Protestants)	Catherine of Aragon
Anne of Cleves (with Germany against Spain)	Jane Seymour	Catherine Howard (with the Catholics)	Anne Boleyn
	Catherine Howard		Jane Seymour
	Catherine Parr		

Catherine of Aragon (Spanish)	Anne Boleyn (English)	Jane Seymour (English)	Anne of Cleves (German)	Catherine Howard (English)	Catherine Parr (English)
To make an alliance with Spain	To have a son	To have a son. To get support from Protestants	To make an alliance with Germany	To get support of English Catholics	To look after Henry as he got old
A daughter, Mary	A daughter, Elizabeth	A son, Edward	No children	No children	No children
Ended in: divorce	Ended in: execution	Ended in: death in childbirth	Ended in: divorce	Ended in: execution	Ended in: Henry's death
Lasted for: 24 years	Lasted for: 3 years	Lasted for: 1 year	Lasted for: 6 months	Lasted for: 2 years	Lasted for: 5 years

PHOTOCOPIABLE

Henry VIII's marriages

Link each of Henry's wives with the reason why Henry married her.
Some reasons apply to more than one wife.
One has been done for you.

Catherine of Aragon

Anne Boleyn

Jane Seymour

Anne of Cleves

Catherine Howard

Catherine Parr

Reasons why Henry married

falling in love

alliance with Spain

alliance with English Protestants

alliance with English Catholics

alliance with Germany

male heir

to look after him in his old age

On the back of this sheet, write why you think Henry VIII married six times.

Name _____

Henry VIII's marriages

Match the sentence starters with the sentence endings to make six correct statements.

Henry VIII married Catherine Parr	to get a son.
Henry VIII married Catherine of Aragon	to get Germany's help against Charles V.
Henry VIII married Anne Boleyn	to gain the friendship of Spain.
Henry VIII married Jane Seymour	to get help from the Protestants.
Henry VIII married Anne of Cleves	to get help from the Catholics in England.
Henry VIII married Catherine Howard	to look after him in his old age.

Now write the statements in the correct order.

1 _____

2 _____

3 _____

4 _____

5 _____

6 _____

On the back of this sheet, write why you think Henry VIII married six times.

Henry VIII's marriages

Next to each of the pictures of Henry's wives, write a sentence to say why he married her. Use information sources to help you.

The Tudor rich

Showcase Tudor houses

The Tudor period was an affluent time for many people. Consequently, there was a huge rise in the number of houses being built and the contents of each house grew accordingly. Focusing on houses and their contents can reveal a tremendous amount about the social history of the Tudor period.

Probably the most famous Tudor property is Henry VIII's palace at Hampton Court (see Generic sheet 2 on page 50). It was initially built for Sir Thomas Wolsey, but he was forced to give it to Henry when he fell out of favour with the king. Wolsey had Hampton Court designed in a similar style to Henry VII's palace at Richmond, with particularly ornate turrets as a key feature. It was located close to the river so that people travelling by boat along the Thames could marvel at the wonderful sight. Henry VIII added the Great Hall and redesigned the Chapel Royal and the Clock Court. The grounds are famous for the maze made from clipped hedges.

The gardens of the rich provided employment for many – from designers to garden boys. With the increase in overseas trade and exploration came the compulsion to grow a wide variety of flowers, trees and shrubs from many different countries. Tudor travellers were always keen to discover interesting plants to bring home, as they were sure to find someone to buy them.

Other well-known examples of fine Tudor architecture are Knole House (Kent), Hatfield House (Hertfordshire), Hardwick Hall (Derbyshire), Longleat House (Wiltshire) and Palmer's Farm – formerly Mary Arden's House – (Stratford-upon-Avon). Smaller mansions and large manor houses sprang up all over the country, easily recognised by the traditional black and white and timber-framed appearance. An example of a smaller mansion is Little Moreton Hall, Cheshire (see Generic sheet 2.

The exterior of Tudor houses

A large number of houses in this period were built in the shape of an 'E' (whether out of respect for Elizabeth I is debatable). The short middle branch of the 'E' was the main entrance porch. The majority of houses were built with a wooden framework (see Generic sheet 3). This was often oak, which has stood the test of time as many of the houses are still around today. Other properties, such as palaces and colleges, were usually built entirely from brick or stone.

In towns, houses could be up to five storeys high. The floorboards of each storey jutted out slightly so the house would gradually lean towards the road. Consequently, the tops of houses in towns were very close to those on the opposite side of the street. The Shambles in York is a good example of this.

The spaces in the oak frame were filled with wattle and daub or with handmade red clay bricks. Wattle was made from the stems of hazel branches woven together. The plaster, also known as daub, was made from clay, lime, cow dung, chopped straw and water. An excellent example of this can be seen at Anne of Cleves' House in Lewes, Sussex. Some windows had glass in the frames, but this was still very expensive. If a person moved to a new house, they sometimes took the windows with them. Houses did not have many windows. Shutters were fastened to the outside to keep out the rain.

The end of a roof and gables were decorated with carved boards. The roof itself would be thatched or tiled. Chimneys were very tall and decorative. At the back of a typical Tudor house, in a strategic corner, could be found the outlet for the garderobe, or toilet (see Generic sheet 3). This was an overhang opening from the first storey emptying down into a waste pit layered with a bed of ashes. When the pit was full, the waste was mixed with more ashes and used as fertiliser for the garden.

The interior of Tudor houses

Wealthy people at this time began to prefer smaller rooms rather than one main room (as in older houses) in which everything happened. Typically there would be a parlour, a dining room and a back kitchen on the ground floor with bedrooms upstairs. The finest room, known as the long gallery, was upstairs, running the whole length of the house. This was where women would walk in their finery if it was too wet to stroll outside in the gardens, and it was an ideal place for children to play or be given lessons by a local priest.

In a palace or extremely rich person's house, there would be a great hall two storeys high with a gallery for musicians or for the women to watch the men dining! There would be a stone fireplace with a decorated fireback. The log fire was held in a pair of brass andirons.

Walls would often be covered in wood panelling called wainscoting. This was usually oak, sometimes painted over. Wall hangings, such as tapestries, could decorate the walls, as could carpets bought from traders in the East. These would never be put on the floor. Carved wood was the predominant feature of the furniture, including doorposts, sideboards and staircases that sometimes had ornate gates at the bottom to keep the dogs downstairs.

Floors were made from stone slabs or tiles, and were covered with rushes or rush mats. Even lavender was known to cover the floor to keep away bad smells. There was also a custom of hanging leafy branches or lavender branches on the walls to act as air fresheners. Lighting was by candles, or rushes soaked in fat and held in holders called rush nips. These holders allowed the rushes to burn at both ends ('burning the candle at both ends'). People in town houses would light a candle at the entrance to their home to light the way for travellers.

There was a general increase in the amount of furniture in each house during the Tudor period. Looking at inventories of property can reveal a great deal about a person, his family and their lifestyle. Four-poster beds with feather mattresses were the height of luxury and were passed from generation to generation; pewter and silver vessels were also a sign of affluence. The contents of the kitchen also reveal many aspects of Tudor life, from everyday dining to lavish feasts.

Whether they lived in a palace, a mansion or a manor house, the rich grew in status throughout the Tudor period. Merchant traders also increased their wealth and often lived in large town houses. It was a period of rapid growth in prosperity.

Inventories were kept by those rich people who had belongings to pass on to their descendants. The longer the inventory, the richer the person.

Inventory for Mr Henry Taylor

2 chairs in the whole house
8 stools and forms
2 square tables
6 bedsteads with tapestry hangings
6 feather mattresses and cushions of velvet and satin
3 great chests
2 carpets
5 cupboards
15 candlesticks
1 fire shovel and tongs
1 basin and pewter jug
6 glasses
6 plates
2 large pewter plates

The Tudor rich

History objectives (Unit 8)
- The key features of Tudor buildings.
- To use inventories to identify characteristic features of different types of people in Tudor times.

Resources

- Generic sheets 1–5 (pages 49–54)
- A board, flip chart or OHP
- Coloured highlighters
- Activity sheets 1–3 (pages 55–57)

Starting points: *whole class*

Show the children the picture of the modern house on Generic sheet 1). Discuss the following questions with them:

- What does this house look like?
- What do you think it is made from?
- How old do you think it is?
- How many rooms might it have?
- What happens in the rooms?

Then show the children a picture of a typical Tudor home (enlarge a picture from Generic sheet 2). Ask them if they can estimate when it was built or if they can say what sort of house it is. Explain briefly what it is made from, using the information from the teachers' notes. Use the following key words: wood, oak, wattle, daub, plaster, strong, storey. Discuss who might have lived in the house in Tudor times (key words: rich, affluent, merchant).

Invite the children to estimate how many rooms there are in the house and what each of the rooms was used for (key words: kitchen, parlour, bedchamber, long gallery, great hall and garedrobe). Generic sheet 3 may be useful.

As a whole class, read 'A guided tour with William' on Generic sheet 4 (see pages 52 and 53). Give the children copies of the story to follow. Discuss what sort of person they think William is, his background, and so on. Explain that they are going to be research detectives to find out things about the homes of rich people in Tudor times. Ask them to underline or highlight in the passage all the different rooms that are mentioned in the story (for

example, parlour and kitchen). Invite the children to give feedback and make a list on the board, flip chart or OHP.

Ask the children to highlight or underline in a different colour all the different possessions that are mentioned in the story. Give examples to guide their research (for example, chairs, table, sideboard, four-poster bed, feather mattress and rush nips). Make a list on the board and then look at the pictures of some of these objects on Generic sheet 5. Ask the children to tell you what they think an inventory is. Look at the objects underlined in the story. Ask the children to help you make an inventory on the board of the items in each room (under room headings).

Tell the children that they are now going to design their own Tudor house and make an inventory of the items inside it.

Group activities

Activity sheet 1
This sheet is for children who need more support. They have to design and label the structural features of a house for a rich Tudor family. Generic sheets 2 and 3 give visual guidance. They have to select items from a given inventory that they think would be found in their Tudor house. Then they have to write what sort of family might have lived in the house.

Activity sheet 2
This sheet is for children who can work independently. They have to design and label the structural features of a house for a rich Tudor family. Generic sheets 2, 3 and 4 will help them. Then they are given three areas of a Tudor home (kitchen, dining room and bedchamber) and have to make an inventory of the items that might be found there. Generic sheets 4 and 5 will help. Then they have to make inferences about the sort of people who might have lived in their Tudor home.

Activity sheet 3

This sheet is for more able children. They have to create and label a design for a rich Tudor house. They have to draw a floor plan and identify the rooms. They have to create an inventory, using Generic sheet 4 for guidance. Then, given a picture of four members of a rich Tudor family, they have to imagine these people live in the Tudor house and write about their lives (making their own inferences about life for the Tudor rich).

Plenary session

Look at the different designs for a Tudor house that the children have created in their group work. What have they all got in common? Some Tudor homes survive to this day. What does this tell the children about the structural features?

Try to piece together an inventory from all the children's ideas using a flip chart, board or OHP. Share their ideas on what sort of person might have lived there. Ask:

• What is the same and what is different about a Tudor house and a modern house?
• Are items missing from the Tudor inventory that you would have expected to see? (More toys, more comfortable seating, more games.)
• Were all inventories the same?
• What can be inferred from an inventory with few items in it? Did it mean the owner was not as wealthy?
• Did having lots of possessions in Tudor times make you a more important person?
• Would you have enjoyed living in a Tudor house? Why? Why not?

Some Tudor houses survive today. What does this tell the children about the external features of a Tudor house? (That it was made from materials strong enough to withstand weather conditions over a long period of time.)

Ideas for support

For children who find it difficult to design a Tudor house rather than a modern house, look carefully with them at Generic sheets 2 and 3.

Ask:

• What do you think the beams were made from?
• Do you think the windows had glass in them?
• Where was the door?
• Where do you think the toilet would be?

Read them relevant parts of Generic sheet 4. Look together at Generic sheet 5.

Some of the items in the inventory on Activity sheet 1 could be both modern and Tudor, so allow the children to make their own decisions.

For the creative writing, ask:

• Do you think the Tudor family enjoyed parties?
• Do you think they had servants to help look after the house?
• Do you think their beds would have been comfortable to sleep in?
• Would you have liked their food and drink?

For more able children, real inventories can be found on websites, CD-Roms and in books. These give clues to rich Tudor lifestyles and help stimulate creative writing.

Ideas for extension

Awareness of external and internal features of Tudor houses will be increased by making scale models using a balsawood frame and papier-mâché walls, possibly trying to use their own version of wattle and daub. Make a display of the models. Include garden designs. More able children could recreate a nearby Tudor house. Internal features could include the different items of furniture in each room, to contrast with the homes of the Tudor poor.

Explore the local community to discover any houses dating back to Tudor times. If possible, arrange a class outing to one of the more famous Tudor homes (see Useful resources on page 117).

Ask the children to write a diary entry for a rich person using inferences from the type of possessions found in a Tudor home. This activity requires further research.

Linked ICT activities

Look at the pictures of the Tudor homes on Generic sheet 2 with the children. Discuss the main features of the buildings (the strong black timber frame and the white walls of the completed building). Look at the different widths of the black timbers; look at how the lines join together and the patterns that are created.

Using a drawing package such as *Dazzle* or Microsoft *Paintbrush*, show the children how to use the straight-line tool and how to change the width of the line they are drawing with. (See Useful resources on page 118.) Using this tool, Generic sheet 2 and other images of Tudor houses for ideas, ask the children to create their own design for the outside of a Tudor house. This is not a 3-D design but a simple 2-D picture, which encourages them to look for patterns in the buildings and to recreate these patterns using a simple line drawing tool.

Show the children how to copy a pattern they have created for part of the house, and how to paste this pattern and use it to form another part of the house.

Print out the final picture and create a class display of a Tudor street.

The Tudor rich

The Tudor rich

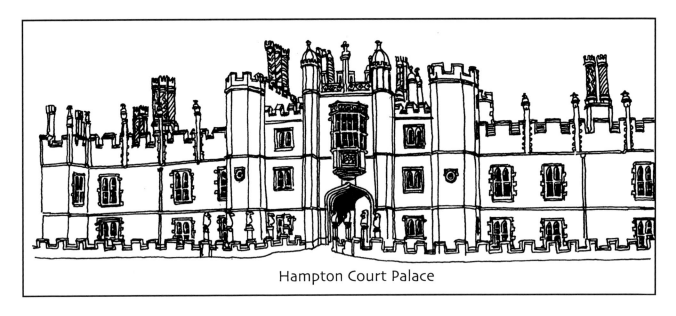

Hampton Court Palace

Little Moreton Hall, Cheshire

Merchant's house, Shrewsbury

Barrington Court, Somerset

The Tudor rich

The wood framework of a Tudor house

Inside a garderobe
(left) and the outside
(below)

The Tudor rich

A guided tour with William

Welcome to my home. My family have lived here for ten years now. I was born here but my older sisters weren't. They were born in our first house in the town, which was much smaller. Our father is a very successful merchant. He is always busy but he makes lots of money so we can have lots of new things in our house. Let me show you round.

This is our parlour. Do you like the wood panelling? I love all the carvings and decorations – I especially like rubbing my hands over them. I'd like to be a wood carver but I suppose I'll have to be a merchant like Father; that's what my teacher says as I am the only son in the family. Because I'm showing you around today I'm not having any lessons so I can have a break from learning my Latin verbs.

This tapestry on the wall is my mother's favourite. My friend, Thomas, hasn't got any tapestries in his house. Isn't the tapestry huge? It covers the whole wall. These chairs are beautifully carved from oak and have got the same pattern on the legs as the table and the sideboard. Be careful as you walk over the rushes on the floor. The maid has not changed them yet today.

Through here is the dining room. We eat our meals here. My favourite meal is blackbird pie. Our cook is very good although she makes us eat lots of vegetables. But she does make great comfits. My elder sister says her kissing comfits are the best for making your breath smell sweeter. I like them because they are really tasty, especially after we've had to eat some of the salted meat. We eat off pewter plates. I'm old enough now to have my own knife and I enjoy drinking my ale out of my own silver cup. Christmas feast is a very special meal. We have so many candles in the silver candlesticks and rush nips everywhere. The carpet on the table at the moment is from the East somewhere. My father brought it home one day. I think it's a bit heavy to keep having to take it off the table when we eat.

Come this way. Mind your head! This is the kitchen. Hello, Cook. Something smells good. It must be the fresh bread baking in the oven next to the big kitchen fire. The brass andirons hold the logs and the meat cooks over the fire on the spit. Molly over there is preparing the vegetables. There are lots of things that could hurt me in here, especially the sharp knives for chopping meat, so I'm not allowed to stay for too long, but it is always a warm and friendly place.

Back out we go, up the stairs. Follow me. I love this wooden staircase, especially the carvings on the stair gates. When Father brings the dogs in, we put the gates across because we don't want them up here. This is the long gallery. Isn't it huge? It is the full length of the house. I love playing up here. This is where I have my lessons, too. Mother likes to walk up here with her friends and look out at our beautiful garden. Come and have a look. Mind yourself; there is glass in these windows. You can just see John the gardener at the far end of the lawn, down near the river. He's so far away he looks like a spider. The trees are my favourites. I would love to climb to the top and see for such a long way. Still, I'm good at playing skittles down there on the lawn.

Through here we have the main bedchamber. The four-poster bed is quite old now; it has been in the family for years. My father has just bought a feather mattress for it, but I think he prefers the old straw one. He is always complaining of aching bones at breakfast time. This is the cradle I used to sleep in. That big wooden chest is full of material like the curtains around my parents' bed. Through here is another bedchamber. I sleep on a truckle bed, which is kept under that big bed. These are some of my toys and schoolbooks. Over there is my jug and basin where I have a wash. In my bedchamber you can see the timbers of the frame of the house. They aren't covered with wood panelling or tapestries. I like the patterns of the beams; it makes me feel that this is a very strong house. Look over here; you can see some of the straw bits that are in the plaster between the beams. I think these darker patches in the plaster are bits of clay and cow dung mixed together. I know there is lime mixed with it.

If you need to go to the garderobe, that's along the corridor, back through my parents' bedchamber and through that door. We don't have to go outside like at my friend Thomas's house. Be careful not to drop anything important into the ash pit, which you can see if you look through the hole you sit on. The ash pit was only emptied yesterday so it will be a long time before we can get anything out again. When the gardener spreads the muck to make the flowers grow he finds some interesting things that have been dropped down!

So, we are at the end of the tour. When my father dies we will have to make a list of all that belongs to him. It is called an inventory. The one we got from his father was very short, but I'm sure my father has got a lot more to pass on to me. I hope that won't be for a long time yet. I love my house. Perhaps I could visit your house one day?

The Tudor rich

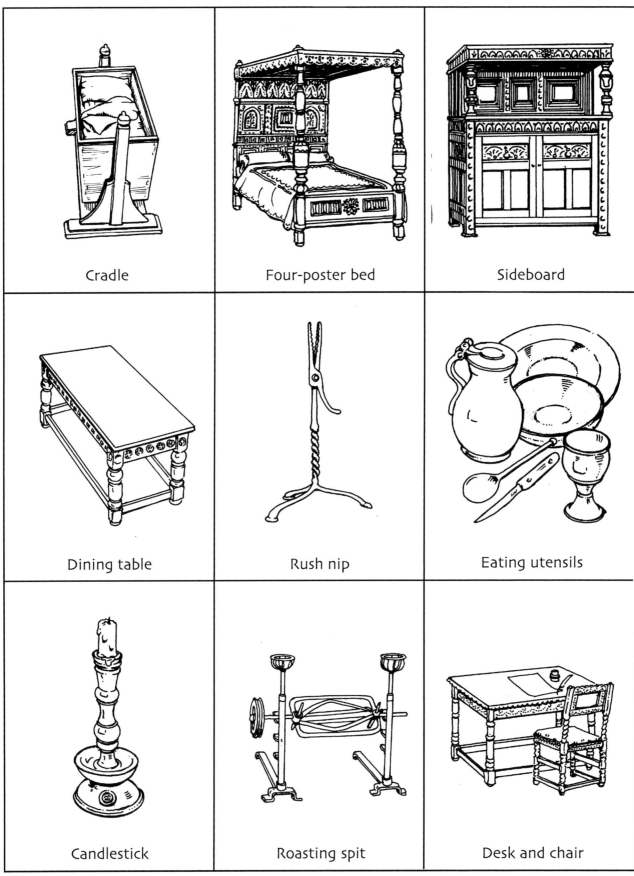

Cradle	Four-poster bed	Sideboard
Dining table	Rush nip	Eating utensils
Candlestick	Roasting spit	Desk and chair

PHOTOCOPIABLE

Name _____

The Tudor rich

Draw a design for a house for a rich Tudor family. Label it, remembering to include wood beams, windows and a large entrance door. If your house has a second floor, make sure it overhangs the ground floor.

- Where will you put the garderobe?
- Is the roof thatched?
- Where is the chimney?

Look at the inventory below. Highlight the items you think could be found in a rich Tudor house.

> 2 large wooden chairs
> 2 carpets
> 4 tapestries
> 1 computer
> 12 light bulbs
> 12 candle holders
> 1 large wooden table
> 1 washing machine
> 2 four-poster beds
> 2 pewter plates
> 6 china plates
> 4 pewter tankards
> 6 drinking glasses
> 1 television

- What sort of family might have lived in your Tudor house?
- Do you think they enjoyed living there?
- What games do you think the children played?
- What sort of food do you think they ate?
- Do you think they had servants to help look after the house?

On the back of this sheet, write your ideas.

Name _____

The Tudor rich

Draw a design for a house for a rich Tudor family. Label it.
Label the rooms in the house.

Complete the inventory below by adding items that you think could be found in
your Tudor home.

Kitchen	Dining room	Bedchamber
cooking pot	dining table	mattress
serving dishes	pewter plates	cabinet

On the back of this sheet, write five sentences about the people who might live in
your Tudor house.

- What might the children do?
- Do you think they enjoyed living in their home?
- Do you think the family had servants to help look after the house?

Name _____

The Tudor rich

Draw a design for a house for a rich Tudor family. Draw a floor plan as well.
Label the house, including the rooms.

On the back of this sheet, write a detailed inventory of the items in your
Tudor house. You could organise it by each room, or by type of item.
Use Generic sheet 4, books and CD-Roms to help you.

Imagine these people living in your Tudor house. On the back of this sheet,
write a paragraph about each person. What sort of things did they do?
What did they enjoy?

The Tudor poor

Life for the poor

While inventories tell us much about the life of the rich, it is a lot harder to find out what life was like for the poor in Tudor times. Unlike richer people, poor people did not have wills or inventories and their homes barely survived their lifetime. All the information we have about poor people is gleaned from sources that describe how others saw them rather than their own opinions and observations. We can only guess and make assumptions at what life was like for such people.

The Tudor poor have been categorised into three main groups:

- those with just enough to live on, such as farm labourers and servants;
- the deserving poor, such as the very young, very old, disabled and widowed;
- those who were fit enough to work but chose not to, such as vagrants; begging was often the only option left for survival.

At the beginning of the Tudor period, the population of England and Wales was quite low because of the aftermath of the Black Death. By the middle of the Tudor period, the population was showing signs of a rapid increase and this, in itself, was creating problems as there were not enough jobs to go round and food was in short supply. Child mortality was still very high amongst the poor. They had roughly the same number of children as the rich, but their babies did well to survive beyond a year.

Concern for the poor was genuine on the part of some of the rich landowners, for a variety of reasons. The main reason was the fear of uprisings from fit, strong, healthy young men who were unable to find work. Some vagabonds had been soldiers and were able to use guns; some even carried them around with them. These men were a potential threat to the rich, who believed the number of vagabonds to be large and their capacity for serious damage to be immense. In reality, the size of this group was probably never very large, or threatening.

The Poor Laws

Throughout the Tudor period, Poor Laws were passed to try to alleviate some of the effects of poverty. The 1601 Poor Law saw the state take responsibility for the poor for the first time. It was to remain in place for the next 300 years until the welfare state was created. Before 1601, the poor were largely the responsibility of the Church. The monasteries played a large part in providing care and provision for the poor but when Henry VIII dissolved them, this provision was cut off. From then on, there was an increase in the variety of Poor Laws passed to try to help. There were two types of Poor Law, those for the 'deserving poor' and those for 'sturdy beggars' or 'vagabonds'.

Almshouses

Almshouses were built by parishes for poor and needy people, particularly those elderly people who had no family to care for them. Often the almshouses were subject to strict rules and regulations, such as regular attendance at church.

A timeline of Tudor Poor Laws

Poor Laws for the deserving poor, who included young orphans, widows with children, the blind, the lame and the elderly, were passed throughout the Tudor period.

- 1495 – the deserving poor could beg in their own parish, but nowhere else.
- 1531 – as in 1495 but they needed a licence from a Justice of the Peace (JP) to do so.
- 1547 – the parish had to provide the deserving poor with a place to live – the funding for this was to be taken from a voluntary collection after church each week. At this time, Edward VI set up Christ's Hospital, St Thomas's Hospital and St Bartholomew's Hospital to help the poor, and Bridewell Prison to punish idlers.
- 1552 – licensed beggars could not sit outside and beg, but they could go from door to door.
- 1563 – those who didn't give money after the church service had to give a reason to a JP. If the reason was insufficient, prison was a possible punishment. The deserving poor had to rely on

the parish handout; only a disabled person could beg from door to door.

- 1597–98 – an overseer was appointed in each parish to organise the care for the poor. Officials set the poor rate and told everyone what they had to give to the overseer for the poor. Those who didn't pay up would lose some of their possessions.

Poor Laws for the 'sturdy beggars' or 'vagabonds' were based on punishments rather than giving any help.

- 1495 – vagabonds, when caught, could be put in the stocks for three days.
- 1531 – vagabonds could be whipped.
- 1536 – vagabonds had to work for the parish in which they were caught, doing jobs such as road repair.
- 1547 – vagabonds were forced to work as slaves (this was too strong a punishment and was stopped in 1549).
- 1572 – vagabonds over the age of 14 could be whipped and a hole put in their right ear to show it was the first time they had been caught. If they were caught again, they could go to prison or even be hanged as a criminal. If they were caught and were aged between 5 and 14, they could be made an apprentice.
- 1576 – the parish had to provide work for vagabonds. If they refused to work, they had to go to the House of Correction in the parish.

- 1597–98 – overseers were in charge of all care, including the running of the House of Correction. Vagabonds who kept getting caught could be sent overseas to work in the colonies.
- 1601 – the responsibility for the poor, whatever their reason for being poor, was put in the hands of the state, not the Church.

The contrast between rich and poor

Poverty came about through:

- lack of food;
- lack of shelter;
- poor health;
- lack of employment.

The rich enjoyed the wealth and prosperity of a thriving nation while the poor lived from hand to mouth, day after day, with no respite from their drudgery. It was a stark contrast in attitude and in strength of mind.

It was rare for poor people to be able to write. Written evidence about them that survives (such as in church and court records) would have been written by educated people who may have had little understanding of or sympathy with the poor. Very few poor homes or possessions survive from the Tudor period. Most evidence about the poor comes from the few wealthy people who did try to help them.

The Tudor poor

History objectives (Unit 8)
- About the lives of the poor in Tudor times.
- About the attitudes of wealthier people towards the poor.
- About the types of evidence and gaps in evidence about the poor in this period.

Resources

- Generic sheets 1–4 (pages 62–66)
- A flip chart
- Activity sheets 1–3 (pages 67–69)

Starting points: *whole class*

Ask the children:

- What does it feel like to be hungry?
- What does it feel like to be really cold?
- What does it feel like to be ill?

Invite them to share their ideas. Explain that this was what it was like for poor people in Tudor times, not just now and again, but all the time. What do the children think could be done to help stop the poor from being hungry, cold and sick? Write their answers on a flip chart so that their ideas can be referred to in the plenary session.

Using the information from the teachers' notes, tell the children that there were three groups of poor people in Tudor times:

- those who had just enough to live on, like farm labourers
- those who were orphaned at a young age, or were disabled or very old
- those who were fit enough to work, but chose not to, like vagabonds.

Tell the children that they are going to look at each group in turn.

Give out copies of Generic sheet 1 about Mary and her family. Ask the children which group they fit into. (The first.) Read the story and ask them to imagine what life was like for this family. Ask 'How does this compare with the life of the rich family you looked at before?', 'Do you think the poor home and its inventory would survive today, like some rich Tudor homes?' and 'Why do you think there is so little evidence about the lifestyle of poor

Tudor people?' (Homes would easily burn down; furniture was poor quality; possessions would be sold to buy food in hard times; very few possessions would be passed on to future generations.) Use Generic sheets 2 and 3 for support.

Next read about James on Generic sheet 1. Ask the children which group he fits into. (The second.) Tell them that he would have been helped by the Church through the local parish. Help them explore the fact that blind people had many more difficulties in Tudor times than they do today, by asking 'How are blind people helped today?' Tell them that the Church kept records about disabled people, and some records have been preserved. Some almshouses built by parishes still exist today.

Now read about Robin on Generic sheet 1. Ask the children which group he fits into. (The third.) Show them Generic sheet 4. Tell them that because the poor were punished by the rich, some records remain about the types of punishments and the reasons they were given. Ask 'Do you think these punishments were fair?'

Tell the children that they are now going to recreate a day in the life of a poor Tudor person. They all need copies of Generic sheets 1–4.

Group activities

Activity sheet 1

This sheet is for children who need more support. They have to imagine what life was like for Edward, the eldest son, and write a diary entry for a day in his life. It may contain drawings. Ask:

- What is your home like? What is it made from?
- Where do you sleep? What time do you get up? What time do you go to bed?
- What do you eat?
- What does your family do all day? What do you do?
- What hobbies do you have?

- Do you have holidays? Are you happy?
- What do you want to be when you grow up?

Activity sheet 2

This sheet is for children who can work independently. They have to imagine what life was like for Edward, the eldest son, and write a diary entry for a day in his life. It may contain drawings. Then they have to describe what they think James's life was like and how he felt, using words and drawings.

Activity sheet 3

This sheet is for more able children. They have to imagine what life was like for Edward, the eldest son, and write a diary entry for a day in his life. It may contain drawings. Then they have to imagine the sorts of crimes that Robin (the vagabond) would commit in order to survive, and the punishments he might receive when he was caught.

Plenary session

Revisit the children's ideas about being poor, cold, hungry and ill from the start of the lesson. Ask them about similarities and differences between Tudor times and today: 'Are hospitals and houses different today?', 'Are punishments fairer today?' These are difficult questions and the children's answers will reflect your local community.

Share some of the diary entries the children have written. Recap what evidence really remains about poor Tudor people. Reinforce that this is mostly about what happened to the poor, not about the people themselves; we can only use our imagination to try to recreate what their lives were like.

Ideas for support

For children who find creative writing difficult, read the stories on Generic sheet 1 carefully with them. Ask questions to focus on what life might have been like for Edward. Cartoons or thumbnail sketches might help before they start writing.

More able children may want to look at more evidence for the lives of the disabled poor, or explore further the punishments and the reasons for them. Provide books and access to websites (see Useful resources on pages 117 and 118). The children will find out that there are gaps in the evidence available.

Ideas for extension

To parallel the work on the Tudor rich, the children could construct a poor home using craft materials. The interior contents would be very limited. The children would see that the homes were not built to last, and begin to grasp why so little information or evidence is available now.

Further projects could be carried out on archeological findings on Tudor life, trying to find more primary evidence to support or dispute the material presented in this chapter. Remind the children that new evidence may be biased too.

Children are always interested in crime and punishment, and they could explore this further. Video material could help them act out their own scenarios. Creative writing, poetry, prose or drama always help children get a feel for social history, leading to some understanding of life in different times.

Linked ICT activities

Discuss with the children what they would eat during one day at home, including snacks as well as main meals. Talk to them about what poor children living during the Tudor period would have had to eat. Make two lists on a flip chart or whiteboard showing the food eaten by children then and food eaten by children today. Talk to them about how the Tudors would have cooked their food, then compare this with the modern technology we have for cooking today.

Talk to the children about the variety of food we have available to us today. Tell them that they are going to use the computer to create a menu for the school canteen. They are going to choose five new snacks, five new main courses and five new puddings for their menu. Show the children some examples of menus from restaurants and cafés. They could also make a menu for a Tudor meal.

Working in pairs and using a word processing or desktop publishing program such as *Textease*, Microsoft *Publisher* or Microsoft *Word* (see Useful resources on page 118), show the children how to insert clip art on the page and how to add text.

The Tudor poor

Mary and her family

Mary lives in the country. She is married to Tom, who works as a farm labourer for the local landowner. They live in a small wattle and daub cottage provided by the landowner. Their children are Edward, aged nine, Ann, aged eight, and baby Jane, aged six months. Mary has had the sadness of two of her children dying from ill health before they were one year old.

Their home is a one-room cottage with a small plot of land where Mary grows carrots and turnips and keeps six hens. Mary cooks over an open fire and the smoke from it goes out through a hole in the roof. There is not much room for them all in the cottage. Edward and Ann sleep in one corner on a bed of straw. Mary and Tom sleep in another corner with the baby next to them.

The baby is not very well and Mary thinks she may die. She is giving her herbs to try to make her better but baby Jane is still very sick.

Ann helps her mother in the house and in the garden but she knows she will soon have to go to work at the landowner's house as a servant. Then she won't see her family very much as she will not get much time to herself.

Edward helps his father on the farm, especially at harvest time, but it is very hard work and he would really like to learn to read and write. His hardest job is when he helps his father move the sheep from one enclosure to the next because some of the local people argue that the land is their common land and they have no right to graze the landowner's sheep there.

Mary and her family are poor, but they are proud that they do not have to ask the parish to give them help. They will manage somehow on Tom's wages. At least they have a home to live in while Tom is working.

James

James can be found in the local town. He has been blind since birth. He is now 19 years old and has discovered the power of ale drinking. It makes him forget about his disability and for a few short hours he is warm from being in the inn where there is always lots of noise and merriment.

In the daytime he begs for food and money from any of the people passing by on their way to the market in the centre of the town. He sleeps wherever he can.

Sometimes the parish will give him shelter and some different clothes to wear, but James doesn't like charity and would prefer to look after himself. He sometimes gets so drunk that he ends up getting into trouble with the local Justice of the Peace.

What he would really like is a wife to look after him and a little cottage to live in with her. Sadly, because of his disability, he resigns himself to a life of survival. His one ray of hope is that he may get a room in the new almshouses that are being built in the town. That depends on the overseer looking kindly on his disability.

Robin

Robin is a crafty, clever man who is 25 years old. He has survived being put in the stocks on numerous occasions in many different towns. But he just keeps moving on, keeping one step ahead. He has a few friends who join him, living at the moment in the woods just outside the town and near enough to the local farmer's land.

He now has the choice of stealing in the town from the rich merchants' houses (sometimes using a long pole to hook things through the open windows) or stealing some of the chickens from the farmer. Either way, he has some excitement in his life, even if he hasn't got a permanent place to live and has no family of his own. He did have a wife and two children but he left them long ago.

His best friend, Thomas, is an old soldier and has his own gun. He has promised to teach Robin how to use it. They might frighten some of the rich men and demand their money. On their travels they have come across tinkers, beggars and many vagabonds like themselves.

The Tudor poor

Words and phrases to describe a poor person's home

Small, draughty, cramped, one room.
Made from wood and thatch – often burned down.
Very poor homes made from mud and branches.
No chimneys.
Fire on hearthstone with smoke going out through a hole in the roof.
Floor of earth beaten flat, sometimes hardened with bull's blood and covered in straw.
Very little furniture – most important item was the cooking pot.
All meals were cooked in this one pot.
Bread and porridge were the main foods, with very weak beer to drink.
Beds were sacks filled with straw.

Almshouses

PHOTOCOPIABLE

The Tudor poor

The poor at work

Ploughing the fields

A beggar

A poor labourer

PHOTOCOPIABLE

The Tudor poor

Punishments

Robbers – one or both ears cut off and nose split open
Sheep stealers – hands cut off
Vagabonds – whipped or put in stocks
Scolds (women who argued or told lies) – ducking stool
Beggars – pillory or branded with a red-hot iron

Whipping in the street

Ducking stool

The pillory

The stocks

PHOTOCOPIABLE

Name _____

The Tudor poor

Imagine what life was like for Edward, the eldest son of the poor family.
Use Generic sheet 1 to help you write a diary entry for one day of Edward's life.

A day in the life of Edward

My house is _____

It is made from _____ and _____

It has _____ room. I sleep _____

I go to bed at _____ o'clock and get up at _____ o'clock.

For breakfast I eat _____ and _____

Today, I _____

_____

_____

_____

_____

_____

_____

The Tudor poor

Imagine what life was like for Edward, the eldest son of the poor family.
Use Generic sheet 1 to help you write a diary entry for one day of Edward's life.

A day in the life of Edward

James

On the back of this sheet, describe what you think James's life was like. How do you think he felt?
Use words and pictures.
Use Generic sheets 1 and 3 to help you.

The Tudor poor

Imagine what life was like for Edward, the eldest son of the poor family.
Use Generic sheet 1 to help you create a diary entry for one day of Edward's life.

A day in the life of Edward

Imagine the sort of crimes that Robin would get up to in order to survive.
On the back of this sheet, write about them.
Describe what punishments he might receive. Include some drawings.

Robin

CHAPTER 7

Making comparisons

Drawing contrasts and comparisons

A lot of background information has been covered in the previous two chapters. The aim here is to use this information and compare it with life in the developed world today. There is potential for many interpretations of this topic and therefore this chapter focuses on four key areas:

- housing;
- possessions;
- lifestyles;
- punishments.

Housing: summary

Comparison of rich and poor in Tudor times
The houses of the rich were made from wood beams and wattle or bricks, whereas the poorest houses were often made from branches and mud. Rich houses were either in towns or with their own gardens in the country. Poor houses were located wherever the landowner chose to build labourers' cottages or in the woods and forests in the country. Poor houses in towns were often built very close together. Rich houses had rooms for specific purposes whereas poor houses had one main room for all purposes.

Modern housing
Modern houses vary in style and design, the majority being made from bricks and mortar. They can be found in towns and in the countryside. Housing types vary from bungalows to high-rise flats, detached and semi-detached, multi-roomed mansions to bedsits.

Comparison of Tudor and modern housing
Rich Tudor houses and modern houses are similar in that rooms are allocated for a purpose, such as eating or sleeping. They are both built to last and are found in similar locations. Poor housing in Tudor times has little in common with housing today due to the state taking responsibility for the provision of adequate housing for all in the form of council or housing trust ownership. The poor in Tudor times may have lived in almshouses and farm labourers may have lived in property owned by the farmer. This form of tied accommodation is still in use today, although the facilities are modernised.

Possessions: summary

Comparison of rich and poor in Tudor times
The poor often had a mattress of straw and a cooking pot as their main possessions, with some tools of their trade as luxury items. The rich had many items for each allocated room, such as a four-poster bed, a sideboard, a dining table, chairs, pewter tableware and an abundance of kitchen utensils.

Modern possessions
Where to begin! The possessions of people today, whether rich or poor, create an endless list, including satellite television, microwave ovens, washing machines and wardrobes.

Comparison of Tudor and modern possessions
This comparison is governed by similarities with the rich Tudor and modern person. The differences begin when the rich Tudor possessions list is exhausted and the modern list keeps on going.

Lifestyles: summary

Comparison of rich and poor in Tudor times
- Rich Tudor people wore many layers of clothing made from fine material with fashionable designs, especially in the hat, shoe and accessory departments. Poor people wore clothes that were practical and functional and often had only the set of clothes they were wearing.
- Food for the poor rarely included meat and was always cooked in one central pot whereas the rich had a varied diet and enjoyed rich feasts.
- The health of the rich tended to be better than that of the poor, probably because of the better diet and because they could afford medical help. Poor people relied on their knowledge of herbs for cures.
- Hygiene was not a major issue for either rich or poor in Tudor times. The rich probably washed more regularly and occasionally took a hot bath. The poor probably bathed in the local stream in their rare moments of relaxation.

- The rich had time for sport, music and art. The poor had very little leisure time if they were working. If they were vagabonds, their pleasure came from their stealing, robbing and general camaraderie.

Modern lifestyles

- Modern people have a choice of clothing, and accessories play a large part in appearance.
- Food is varied and of differing nutritional value. It comes from all over the world.
- Health standards are high, although there are problems related to modern lifestyles, such as obesity, asthma, cancer and AIDS.
- High standards of hygiene are available for all regardless of wealth.
- Entertainment is focused around sport, music, television, theatre, dining out and the internet.

Comparison of Tudor and modern lifestyles

The Tudor lifestyle for the rich compares favourably with the modern lifestyle other than the much wider choice of all things available to the modern person. The lifestyle of the poor in Tudor times was a lot harsher than that of people on low incomes in the developed world. However, it is possible to see a correlation with the poorer developing nations of the world. This is an aspect of the subject that could be developed by older children.

Punishments: summary

Comparison of rich and poor in Tudor times

Wealthy Tudor people gave out the punishments and the poor received them. This seems to represent a 'them and us' mentality. The rich were punished in court and were affected materially whereas the poor were humiliated in their physical punishments.

Modern punishments

Modern punishments tend to be aimed at the financial and materialistic levels of all members of a developed society. Physical punishments still occur around the world.

Comparison of Tudor and modern punishments

Punishments for the rich Tudors affected their wealth – this is the same for the modern person who is fined by a court. Imprisonment is still a well-used option as is the removal of possessions. The biggest difference is that today there are fewer physical punishments, which the poor people of Tudor times endured.

Making comparisons

History objectives (Unit 8)
- To summarise all they have learned about the rich and the poor in Tudor times.
- To select, organise and structure information to answer a key question.
- To distinguish between wealth and poverty in Tudor times.

Resources
- Generic sheets 1–3 (pages 74–76)
- Activity sheets 1–3 (pages 77–79)
- Board or flip chart
- OHP or interactive whiteboard

Starting points: *whole class*

Have a class discussion about life today. Structure the discussion around the following headings:

- Housing
- Possessions
- Lifestyles
- Punishments

Use the board or flip chart to compile four lists of words that the children suggest. For example, housing could include words such as palace, cottage, flat, semi-detached house, bungalow, caravan, tent, sheltered accommodation and old people's home. Possessions should provide an endless list from television to telephone, furniture to microwave oven. Lifestyles can include almost anything else – such as leisure, hobbies, food, drink and clothes. Punishments can range from school punishment to life imprisonment.

Use the three grids on Generic sheets 1 to 3 on an OHP or interactive whiteboard to extend the discussion to comparisons between the Tudor period and today. Use the questions at the bottom of each grid to develop the children's understanding further.

Encourage the children to discuss the comparisons as a whole class, and invite volunteers to fill in various cells of the grids with notes or simple pictures.

Tell the children that they are now going to make their own comparisons between Tudor life and modern-day life.

Group activities

Activity sheet 1
This sheet is for children who need more support. They have to fill in the words in two given paragraphs: a summary of the lives of rich people in Tudor times and a summary of the lives of poor people. On the back of the sheet, they have to give their opinion on why life is better today.

Activity sheet 2
This sheet is for children who can work independently. Using given key words, they have to write what they think are the main advantages of being rich in Tudor times, as well as the main disadvantages of being poor. Then they have to give three reasons why they would choose to live as a rich or a poor person in the period and three reasons why life is better today.

Activity sheet 3
This sheet is for more able children. They have to complete a chart summarising the advantages of being rich and the disadvantages of being poor in Tudor times. Using this information, they have to write a paragraph to answer two questions. Then they have to give three reasons why they would choose to live as a rich or a poor person in the period and answer the question 'Why is life better today?'

Plenary session

Hold a summary discussion of the issues raised in the lesson and on the activity sheets. Encourage the children to express their opinions when discussing the questions of advantages, disadvantages and life today. Summarise the things learned about life in Tudor times.

Ideas for support

Remind the children of the work they have done on rich and poor people in Tudor times. Provide illustrations and word pictures to give them clues. Encourage them to express their own opinions.

Ideas for extension

Use drama to help the children to 'feel' their history; any plays or poems that they write can be acted out or performed in assembly or to parents.

Using an existing town plan, help the children imagine what an area would have been like in Tudor times (rich merchants' houses close together, street traders, beggars, stocks or pillory, poor homes in the woods on the outskirts). Tell the children that there were also lots of people, such as craftsmen and shopkeepers, who were considered neither rich nor poor. Issues such as drainage and water supply, sanitation and health could all be discussed. Make comparisons with the modern town plan. Ask the children to draw a plan of their own Tudor village, town or city.

Linked ICT activities

Discuss with the children how their lives are different from the lives of Tudor children. Talk about some of the daily activities we take for granted (such as watching television), that would not have been available to Tudor children.

Talk about how technology has changed people's lives over the centuries. Make a list with the children of all the possessions they have in their homes that require technology to make them work (washing machines, videos, computers, vacuum cleaners, and so on). Discuss with them how their and their families' lives would be different without the technology.

Tell the children that they are going to use a word processing program to complete a diary for a typical Saturday or Sunday at home.

Ask them to create a list of all the items they used during the diary day that use today's technology. Remind them about the list that the class made earlier.

Using their list of items, ask the children to write a sentence alongside each object describing how they would have carried out the activity in Tudor times. (Telephone: I would have to find the person and talk to them. Television: I would go to watch a play, or find something to play with, or play with my friends.)

Making comparisons

Fill in this chart to show the differences and similarities between Tudor homes (rich and poor) and modern homes.

	Tudor houses		Modern houses
	Rich	Poor	
What are the houses made from?			
Where are the houses built? (Towns, woods, near farms, near water.)			
How many rooms are there in the houses?			
What possessions are there in the houses?			

- What facts are the same for both rich and poor Tudor houses and their contents?
- Give two facts that are different for rich and poor Tudor houses and their contents.
- What is the biggest difference between modern houses and their contents and Tudor houses and their contents?
- Give two facts that are the same for both Tudor and modern housing.

Making comparisons

Fill in this chart to show the differences and similarities between Tudor lifestyles (rich and poor) and modern lifestyles.

| | Tudor lifestyles | | Modern lifestyles |
	Rich	Poor	
Clothes			
Food/drink			
Health			
Hygiene			
Leisure			

- Suggest two reasons why illnesses are different today.
- Do we have more hobbies and pastimes? Why?
- Give two facts that are the same for Tudor and modern lifestyles.

Making comparisons

Fill in this chart to show the differences and similarities between
Tudor punishments and modern punishments.

	Tudor punishments	Modern punishments
Stealing		
Robbing		
Living rough (without a permanent home)		
Telling lies		
Not paying taxes		
Vandalism		

- Which punishments are no longer in use today that were important in Tudor times?
- What modern crimes would not have been a problem in Tudor times?

Name _____

Making comparisons

What were the main advantages of being rich in Tudor times?
Use these words to fill in the gaps in the passage below.

house	cook	teacher	four-poster bed
tankard	meat	ale	pewter

One of the advantages of being rich in Tudor times was living in a large _____ made from strong wood beams and either brick or daub. In your bedroom you might have a _____-_____ _____ with a feather mattress. The _____ would make all your meals and you would eat your _____ and vegetables from a _____ plate, and drink your _____ from a _____. You would either go to school or have a _____ at home.

What were the main disadvantages of being poor in Tudor times?
Use these words to fill in the gaps in the passage below:

hungry	warm	twigs	work	stole
starving	fire	forest	cooking pot	

If you were poor in Tudor times, you might often be cold and _____. Your home may have been made from _____ and straw, and covered in mud, and be in the middle of a _____. The floor would be very hard and you would only have straw in sacks to sleep on. The food would all be cooked in one _____ _____ over a smoky _____. Your clothes would not keep you _____ in the winter and there would not be much _____ to do to keep you busy. If you _____ food because you were _____ you would be punished if you were caught.

On the back of this sheet, write why you think life today is better than in Tudor times.

Making comparisons

What do you think were the main advantages of being rich in Tudor times?
Use the following key words and phrases to help you.
Write your ideas on the back of this sheet.

Houses	Possessions	Lifestyle
rooms	four-poster bed	school
bricks	feather mattress	fine clothes
wood beams	pewter	warmth
thatched roof	fire	walking
chimney	oven	riding
	tapestries	games
	table and chairs	food
		cooks

What were the main disadvantages of being poor in Tudor times?
Use the following key words and phrases to help you.
Write your ideas on the back of this sheet.

Houses	Possessions	Lifestyle
twigs	cooking pot	lack of food
mud	straw mattress	hungry
forest		cold
branches		hard, physical work
		punishments

On the back of this sheet, answer the following questions. Give three reasons for each answer.

- Would you have liked to live at this time as a rich or a poor person?
- Why is life better today?

PHOTOCOPIABLE

Name _____

Making comparisons

What were the main advantages of being rich in Tudor times?
Use these headings to help you.

Houses	Possessions	Lifestyle

On the back of this sheet, use this information to write a paragraph about the main advantages of being rich in Tudor times.

What were the main disadvantages of being poor in Tudor times?
Use these headings to help you.

Houses	Possessions	Lifestyle

On the back of this sheet, use this information to write a paragraph about the main disadvantages of being poor in Tudor times.

On the back of this sheet, write a paragraph to answer each of the following questions. Give three reasons for each answer.

- Would you have liked to live at this time as a rich or a poor person?
- Why is life better today?

CHAPTER 8

Tudor exploration

The beginnings of exploration

One of the main achievements of the Tudor explorers was to prove that the world is round and not flat, as represented in the maps of the Middle Ages. Maps from the Middle Ages focused on Jerusalem as the centre of the Earth, which consisted of the Eastern Mediterranean coastline, North Africa and Europe. It was during the Crusades that educated people began to realise, especially when they met up with Turks and Arabs, that the world extended beyond Europe. The Arabs were excellent traders and had travelled great distances on land by camel and on sea by merchant ships, using stars to navigate.

The Italians were the first to take advantage of Arab knowledge, sending explorers like Marco Polo to the East to trade. In the fifteenth century, the Turks prevented European traders travelling through their empire en route to the East and this posed a problem that was to affect all explorers during the Tudor period. The resulting question was how to reach the East – by sailing south or west? The Portuguese went south along the coast of Africa until Vasco Da Gama sailed round the Cape of Good Hope in 1497 (he went on to control trade as far away as Japan). The Spanish, on the other hand, went west, led by Christopher Columbus (an Italian who tried unsuccessfully to get Henry VII to fund his exploration). Columbus thought the globe was much smaller than it actually is, so when he landed in North America, he was convinced he was in the Indies of the East. He called the locals Indians and the area the West Indies.

Finding and navigating new routes

To take a western route to reach the East raised a new dilemma – should explorers take the South West Passage or the North West Passage to get round America? The Spanish were dominant in this area of exploration, with Magellan and his crew getting the furthest and returning home victorious. Up to this point, the English had not been involved. But in 1497, an Italian, Giovanni Caboto (known to the English as John Cabot) persuaded Bristol merchants to finance him to find the North West Passage around America. Henry VII was also a

backer. As it turns out, Cabot didn't get as far as the East, but he did set up the first English colony in Newfoundland where there was great trade to be had in the fishing industry. English sailors and explorers (Sir Martin Frobisher, Sir Humphrey Gilbert, John Davis, William Balfour, John Bylot) dominated the North West Passage throughout the sixteenth century, but all were unsuccessful. Some thought they were out in the open sea only to find they were actually in a great river, such as the Hudson.

The dominance of Spain over some of the richest parts of South America became obvious during this time. Some English sailors started trading with the Spanish colonies rather than carry on exploring. The Spanish authorities didn't like this and protected their ports with cumbersome galleons. Men such as Sir John Hawkins and Sir Francis Drake used new fast ships to get past the galleons and into the ports to trade or plunder.

Henry VIII was drawn to the idea of sailing and exploration. He set up Trinity House for pilots and built dockyards at Woolwich and Deptford. In 1520, he made a personal voyage to France in *Great Harry*. During Henry's reign, William Hawkins sailed to Guinea in West Africa. Later, in Elizabeth I's reign, Hawkins' son, Sir John Hawkins, became an early slave trader, transporting captives from West Africa across the Atlantic Ocean to sell them to the Spaniards for work on the sugar plantations and in the silver mines.

During Elizabeth I's reign, exploration was at its height. Sir Martin Frobisher was dispatched to find a route to Cathay (China) by sailing north around America. He tried and failed three times, defeated by icy seas. John Davis also tried and failed. (There is a way through the ice, but not for trading ships.)

International trade

The son of John Cabot, Sebastian, was a mapmaker who claimed he had explored the American coast as far as Florida. He set up the Merchant Venturers Company, which sent Sir Hugh Willoughby to find the North East Passage to India going round Lapland and Russia. He failed, but his chief officer,

Richard Chancellor, reached Moscow and successfully traded with the Russians. The Russians wanted English cloth and weapons and the English wanted Russian furs, hemp for ships' ropes, and tallow for candles and soap. The Muscovy Company was set up with regular trade taking place.

England was becoming known as a trading nation. During Elizabeth I's reign, the conflict between Spain and England increased with English sea captains, such as Hawkins and Drake, attacking Spanish bases in America and the West Indies.

As well as exploring and trading by sea, expeditions went overland. Ralph Fitch travelled overland to China. After eight years away, he came back to tell of strange new lands and great opportunities to trade in spices, cloth and rare Eastern goods. To encourage this, on 31 December 1600, Elizabeth granted a charter to the East India Company. There was a lot of rivalry for this lucrative trade, especially from the Dutch, but gradually the East India Company grew in stature and success.

Settlements

The other famous explorer of Elizabethan times was Sir Walter Raleigh. He was one of Elizabeth's favourites and she did not allow him to go exploring until he married and fell out of favour. It was during the 1580s that settlements were being considered in North America. In Central and South America the Spaniards had settled successfully.

Raleigh became involved in these North American settlements, calling one of the new lands Virginia, after the Virgin Queen Elizabeth. The first attempt at settlement in Roanoke, North Carolina, took place in 1585. It was not successful until James I's reign.

Raleigh dreamed of expeditions to the New World in the hope of discovering gold in El Dorado – the land of gold. When he finally set sail in 1595, he only returned with quartz with specks of gold in it. Unfortunately, Raleigh was not liked by Elizabeth's successor and he ended up in the Tower of London for 13 years. In 1617 he was given permission to go to South America to find gold. He failed and was involved in skirmishes with the Spanish. James I was so angry with Raleigh that he had him executed, which made him a people's hero.

Reasons for exploration

The Tudors were motivated to explore for the following reasons.

- To find new locations for trading and therefore to increase the import and export profits of England.
- To discover new routes to get to these trading centres (and hopefully to do so before other European countries).
- To take settlers to new countries to increase English influence abroad.
- To fight and win battles at sea to increase English dominance on the seas.

Tudor exploration

History objectives (Unit 19)
- To compare the knowledge of the world that people had in Tudor times with what is known today.
- The context of the voyages of Tudor explorers.
- That exploration in the sixteenth century led to better knowledge of the world.

Resources

- Generic sheets 1–3 (pages 85–87)
- Smart board (optional)
- Activity sheets 1–3 (pages 88–90)
- Coloured pens
- An atlas

Starting points: *whole class*

Ask the children to close their eyes and remember the very first day they walked into school. How did they feel? Were they nervous because they didn't know what to expect? Were they quite confident because they already knew someone who attended the school who had talked positively about it? Was it a big risk to take or had their parents reassured them? Stepping out into the unknown is something we all sometimes have to do. Encourage them to remember other occasions when they went somewhere new for the first time – for example, to a holiday resort or an activity club.

Ask the children to keep those ideas and feelings in their minds but to now open their eyes and try to answer the following questions. The greatest journey of exploration in modern history was to the Moon. Ask the children how they think the first astronauts felt when they set out. Would they have confidence in their spacecraft? Would they have confidence in their back-up team on Earth? Was it a big risk to take? Let the children know that it doesn't matter how big or small the first step of discovery is, whether it be stepping out on the Moon or exploring a new school for the first time, the feelings are very similar.

Explain to the children that they are now going to go back in time to discover something about the explorations and discoveries made in Tudor times. Together, look at the first known map of the world (c550BC) by Anaximander on Generic sheet 1. Discuss what the children can see on the map. What countries are recognisable? Which continents

are labelled? Why was the Mediterranean area quite accurate in outline? (Because Anaximander was a Greek and knew his own area.)

Then show the children the map of the world in 1607 on Generic sheet 2. (This is just after the end of the Tudor period.) Discuss what they can see on the map. Which countries are recognisable? What is different about the shape of the land drawn? (It is misshapen.) Ask the children to list the continents they can see on the map. (If a Smart board is available, the map can be found on the University of Yale website – see Useful resources on page 118 – providing a clear visual image for children to explore. A map from 1565 can be found on the National Geographic website.)

Some countries had not been discovered in Tudor times; just as today, there are areas of the world still to be explored in detail and areas of the universe still unexplored even with a telescope. But we can tell from these old maps that in Tudor times there was still a lot of our world to discover and explore. Look at the modern map of the world in an atlas and see if it is possible to work out which countries or continents were unknown in the Tudor period.

Give the children copies of the list of Tudor explorers on Generic sheet 3. Ask them to use the map on Generic sheet 2 to find out where the explorers travelled to and the routes that they took. A modern atlas will help to locate the countries. Discuss some of the difficulties the explorers might have faced, such as crossing oceans, following a strange coastline, inclement weather, inadequate ships and fear of the unknown.

Tell the children that they are now going to complete an activity sheet comparing Tudor travel with travel today.

Group activities

Activity sheet 1

This sheet is for children who need more support. On the outline map from Tudor times they have to lightly colour in the continents and oceans. Then they have to mark Raleigh's travel route and estimate how long the sea journey took. (Several months.) On a modern map, they again use colour to distinguish between land and sea. The route they have to colour in is from England to Florida. Then they have to estimate how long it would take to travel by sea (6 days) and by air (9 hours). On the back of the sheet, they list differences between the two maps.

Activity sheet 2

This sheet is for children who can work independently. They also use light colours to distinguish between land and sea and then mark travel routes of Raleigh and Cabot. They also have to estimate how long the sea journey took. (Several months.) On the modern map, they again use light colours to distinguish between land and sea and then mark the route from England to Florida. Then they have to estimate how long it would take to travel by sea (6 days) and by air (9 hours). On the back of the sheet, they list differences between the two maps.

Activity sheet 3

This sheet is for more able children. On an outline map from Tudor times they colour the continents and oceans then mark the travel routes of Raleigh, Cabot and Frobisher. (You may choose to ask them to mark additional routes as described on Generic sheet 3.) They estimate how long the sea journey took. (Several months.) On a modern map, they again use colour to distinguish between land and sea and then mark a route from England to a destination of their choice, saying what they would buy there. They estimate how long it would take to travel by sea and by air. They list differences between the two maps and also have to write about the risks taken today, compared with those taken by Tudor explorers.

Plenary session

Ask where the children have travelled outside the UK. Can they find the country on a modern map and on the Tudor map on their activity sheet? How long did it take to get there? Did they know beforehand – perhaps from pictures – what the place would be like? Compare the time taken for a holiday flight (less than a day) with the two months

taken by a Tudor explorer's ship just to cross the Atlantic. Children in Tudor times very rarely went outside their locality, so their knowledge of the world was very limited. How much more do children know of the world today?

Stress the fact that maps would not have become more accurate without the Tudor explorers' voyages. Ask some of the children who completed Activity sheet 3 to share with the class their writing about the risks taken by Tudor explorers. Why do they think these people were willing to take the risks? (Fame, riches, opening trade routes.) Old maps can be confusing and misleading. It is amazing that the early explorers ever survived to tell their tales! Help the children to understand that modern maps make for a much safer journey! Discuss with them their findings from the activities. Do they think that travel times by sea today are faster? Make sure they give reasoned answers. Travel today is the norm; in Tudor times it was a big adventure. Do the children think that the world has become 'smaller'? Are there still areas left to explore? Can they think of a modern 'unmapped world' that will be explored in the future? (The planets and beyond.)

Ideas for support

For children who find it difficult to distinguish between land and sea on a map, talk with them about countries they can recognise easily. Use a modern atlas to compare countries. As they follow the routes taken by the explorers, discuss with them ideas of distance, using examples they can readily grasp, such as 'How long does it take to cross the English Channel by ferry?' (30 minutes from Dover to Calais.) Now imagine crossing the Atlantic Ocean. For children who are expected to plot their own route to a country of their choice, help them to research the trade potential of that country by using internet links.

Ideas for extension

To help the children understand the three-dimensional image of the known Tudor world, show them how to make a globe using papier mâché. They could make their own globes of the Tudor world with known continents clearly labelled.

Cover a large surface area (either on a wall or on a table) with the outline of a Tudor world map and use three-dimensional model ships to illustrate the routes taken by explorers.

Help the children to compare the reasons for exploration in Tudor times with the reasons for exploration in modern times by asking them to draw up a large Venn diagram to be displayed in the classroom. Ask them to put reasons that apply to both Tudor and modern times in the intersecting area of the two circles.

Ask the children to find out more about old maps and what they can tell us about the history of the world, by using the internet.

Modern maps give incredible detail. More able children could research the use of satellite photography to make modern maps more accurate.

Linked ICT activities

Discuss with the children what it is like to go on a journey to another country today. Talk to them about all aspects of the journey, such as making a phone call to book train tickets, visiting the travel agent and booking a hotel or other accommodation. Compare this to the way the explorers in Tudor times might have prepared for their journey.

Talk to them about how modern technology would help explorers setting out on a journey today.

Together list all the different ways in which a computer is used today when planning and going on a journey. Talk about the use of the internet to keep in touch, navigation systems, satellite weather stations and so on. Talk to them about the importance of having this information available and being able to have access to it.

Using *Numberbox* or Microsoft *Excel*, start with a simple example and show the children how to create a spreadsheet that will be used to hold information about passengers taking a trip by plane from the UK to the USA. (See Useful resources on page 118.) Discuss with them the important and sensitive issues surrounding the storage of information, such as data protection.

Tudor exploration

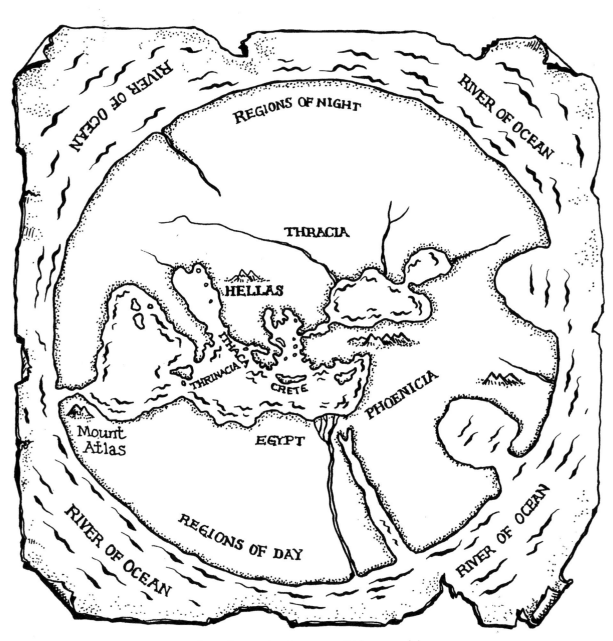

Anaximander's map of the world

This map, made around 550BC, is interesting because it shows that all the land was surrounded by water.

When compared to a modern map of the Mediterranean area it is quite accurate.

Tudor exploration

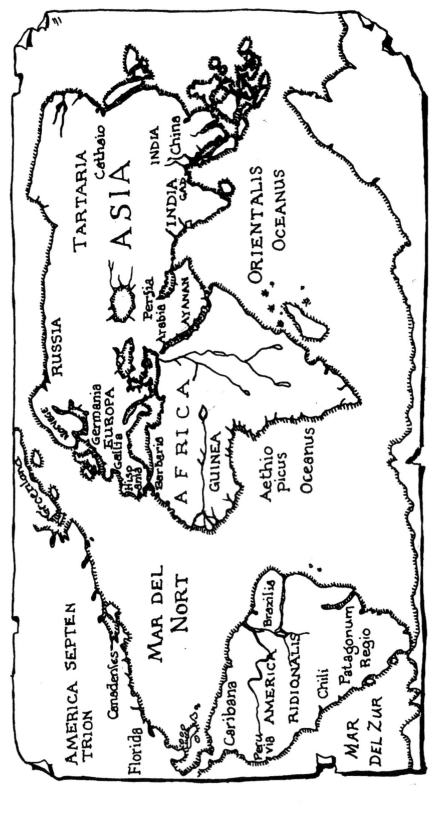

Map of the world, 1607

This map shows an accurate understanding of the explored world. North America is one-sided and Australia has yet to be discovered. South America blends into the South Pole area.

PHOTOCOPIABLE

Tudor exploration

1497

John Cabot set up an English fishing colony in Newfoundland, North America.

Henry VIII's reign

Henry VIII sailed in *Great Harry* to France.

William Hawkins sailed to Guinea in West Africa.

Dockyards set up in Greenwich and Deptford.

Elizabeth I's reign

Sir John Hawkins set up a slave trade between West Africa and the Spanish territories in South America.

Sir Martin Frobisher and **John Davis** tried, and failed, to sail north around America to get to the East.

Sebastian Cabot sailed into Hudson Bay, North America, in 1508. He also explored the coast of Uruguay, South America, in 1527.

Sir Hugh Willoughby and **Richard Chancellor** tried to find the North East Passage to India going round Lapland and Russia in 1553. They failed but Chancellor went overland to meet up with the Russian tsar, Ivan the Terrible, and set up a trade contract that led to the Muscovy Company being formed.

Frobisher explored the Hudson Straits, North America, in 1576.

Ralph Fitch travelled overland to China, eventually leading to the setting up of the East India Company in 1600.

Sir Francis Drake completed his voyage around the world in 1580.

Sir Walter Raleigh discovered Roanoke Island, in North America, in 1584.

A first attempt at settlement in Roanoke took place in 1585.

Raleigh sailed to Guiana, South America, in 1595.

Tudor exploration

Lightly colour in the continents and oceans. Mark the route taken by Raleigh. He travelled by sea. How long do you think it took?

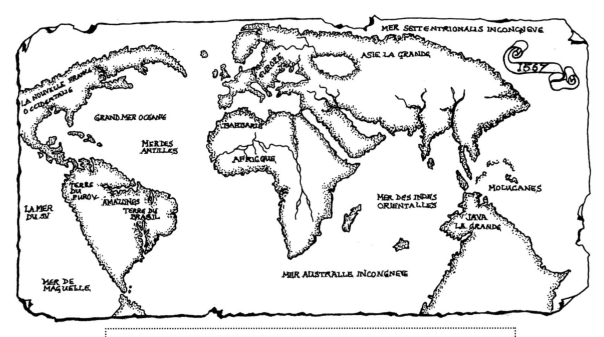

Map of the world as it was known in Tudor times

Lightly colour in the continents and oceans. Colour the route from England to Florida. If you travelled by sea, how long do you think it would take? How long do you think it would take by air?

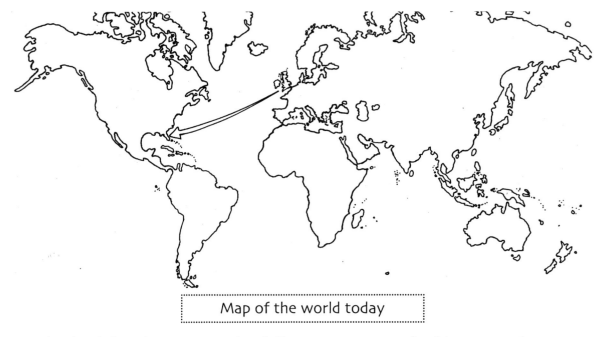

Map of the world today

On the back of this sheet, write the differences you can find between the two maps.

Name _____

Tudor exploration

Lightly colour in the continents and oceans. Mark the routes taken by Raleigh and Cabot. They travelled by sea. How long do you think it took?

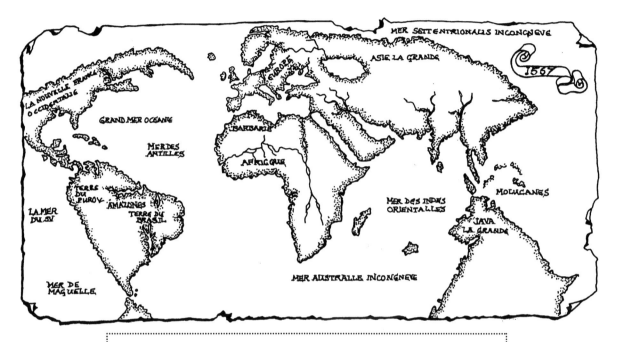

Map of the world as it was known in Tudor times

Lightly colour in the continents and oceans. Draw and colour the route from England to Florida. If you travelled by sea, how long do you think it would take? How long do you think it would take by air?

Map of the world today

On the back of this sheet, write what differences you can find between the two maps.

Tudor exploration

Lightly colour in the continents and oceans. Mark the routes taken by Raleigh, Cabot and Frobisher. They travelled by sea. How long do you think it took?

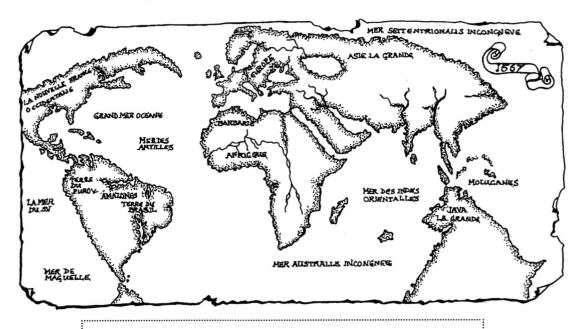

Map of the world as it was known in Tudor times

Lightly colour in the continents and oceans. Imagine you are a modern trader. Choose your own trade route and mark it on the map. What goods are you trading? How long do you think it would take by sea, and how long by air?

Map of the world today

On the back of this sheet, write what differences you can find between the two maps. Then write about the risks Tudor explorers took. Do you think the same risks are taken in travel today?

PHOTOCOPIABLE

Drake's voyage

CHAPTER 9

TEACHERS' NOTES

Sir Francis Drake

Francis Drake (see Generic sheet 1 on page 95) was born the eldest of 12 sons near Tavistock in Devon around 1543. During the reign of Mary Tudor, his family moved to Chatham in Kent to get away from the religious persecution they were suffering in Devon. His father's Protestant preaching had a profound effect on Drake and was to influence the rest of his life. Apparently, he led prayers twice a day throughout the long circumnavigation of the world between 1577 and 1580. Drake had two wives – when he was 25 he married Mary Newman, who died in 1583, and two years later he married Elizabeth Sydenham. There were no children from either marriage. He owned and lived in Buckland Abbey and was Lord Mayor of Plymouth in 1581.

Drake first went to sea as an apprentice on a trading ship based in Chatham. When the owner of the ship died, Drake inherited the ship. He sold it and returned to Devon where he joined forces with his cousin, Sir John Hawkins, to make the first African slave-trading journeys to America.

Success and popularity at the Elizabethan court came with the profitable plundering of Spanish ships. Drake became so bold that he began to attack Spanish and Portuguese ports in South America, using his seaman skills as well as his cunning tactical awareness. On one such voyage to Panama, escaped slaves, called *cimarrones*, who disliked their Spanish oppressors, helped Drake. One *cimarrone*, Diego, worshipped Drake and returned to England with him, later accompanying him on the long voyage around the world.

Circumnavigating the globe

The plan behind the circumnavigation of the globe (see Generic sheets 1 and 2 on pages 95 and 96) was probably to plunder as much gold and riches from the Spanish as possible. The first man to circumnavigate the world successfully was Ferdinand Magellan in 1522. In 1577, Elizabeth I sent Francis Drake and five ships off on their travels with her blessing. The plan was to sail through the Straits of Magellan at the tip of South America.

Elizabeth also gave Drake her secret permission to plunder Spanish ships and ports along the way.

Drake had 164 seamen and five ships: *Pelican* (the largest at 100 tons), *Elizabeth*, *Swan*, *Marigold* and *Benedict*. They sailed from Plymouth, down the west coast of Africa and across the Atlantic, arriving on the coast of South America. Worried that the five ships might get separated, Drake destroyed the *Swan* and the *Benedict*. It is not clear whether or not the seamen actually knew the sort of voyage with which they were involved. Some evidence suggests they thought they were going to plunder ships in the Mediterranean. They spent the winter in Port St Julian and then in September 1578 they passed through the treacherous Straits of Magellan, where the *Marigold* sank with all its crew. The *Elizabeth* then turned back to return to England.

The *Pelican* was renamed the *Golden Hind* (see Generic sheet 3 on page 97) and continued up the west coast of the continent (plundering Spanish ships loaded with gold and treasures from the Incas). It continued north beyond Spanish territory up the unexplored coast of North America. At the state now called California, Drake went ashore, named it New Albion and left behind a sixpence and a metal plaque claiming the land to be a dominion of Queen Elizabeth I.

Drake then had to make a momentous decision – should he go back the way he had come and face the wrath of the Spanish, or should he strike out into the unknown waters of the Pacific Ocean? It was probably a good thing that he underestimated the size of the Pacific Ocean; otherwise he might never have set out to cross it. It took 68 days before land – the Moluccas or Spice Islands (now Indonesia) – was sighted. In June 1580, he reached the Cape of Good Hope in South Africa and sailed on to reach Plymouth, England, in September 1580. Elizabeth I was so pleased to see Drake (and all the wealth he had returned with) that she knighted him on his ship at Deptford on the River Thames. The journey had made a 1400 per cent profit, with riches worth £600,000 (£60 million today). Half of this was given to Elizabeth while Drake was given £10,000.

Striking against Spain

For obvious reasons, Drake's success (and therefore Elizabeth's) did not please the Spanish king, and animosity between England and Spain grew more intense, leading to the attack and defeat of the Spanish Armada.

Drake continued to harass the Spanish, using his skill and bravery to attack whenever needed. The most famous attacks were on the Spanish ports of Cadiz and Corunna in 1587, when many Spanish ships were sunk or captured. To add to this, supplies were destroyed and so the planned Spanish attack on England was delayed. When the attack eventually happened, Drake was Vice Admiral of the Fleet to the Lord High Admiral, Howard of Effingham, and was involved in the English victory.

Fittingly, Drake died at sea (of dysentery) in January 1596, off the coast of Panama. His body was buried at sea in a lead casket. He was about 54 years old.

Drake's voyage

History objectives (Unit 19)
- About the main events in Drake's voyage around the world.
- To appreciate the dangers and discomfort of voyages of exploration.
- To infer reasons why the voyage took place.
- To apply their understanding of chronology.

Resources

- Generic sheets 1–5 (pages 95–99)
- A whiteboard or flip chart
- Activity sheets 1–3 (pages 100–102)
- A globe

Starting points: *whole class*

Discuss the longest journeys the children have been on. What preparations were made before the journey could take place? (Travel arrangements, booking accommodation and arranging spending money, clothing, food, and health insurance.)

Using the information from the teachers' notes and Generic sheets 1 and 2, tell the children the story of Drake's voyage around the world. Ask them to describe Drake, adding their own words to the list on Generic sheet 1. Can they think of other leaders who have a similar character? Would they like to work for that sort of leader? If the journey was going to be such a huge adventure, did it need such a strong character for its leader?

Follow the route on the world map on Generic sheet 1. Emphasise that Drake never turned back; he always went forward.

Using Generic sheets 3 and 4, discuss with the children the sort of ship that the Tudors used – in this instance the ship that Drake sailed in. Ask them to count all the sails. Ask for comments about the amount of rigging needed to keep the sails up for them to be effective. Who do they think did all the hard work of putting the sails up and taking them down? Do they think life was easy for Tudor sailors? Point out the very physical jobs they had to carry out. Generic sheet 5 gives more details about life at sea, as an aid to discussion. The information about measuring the speed of the ship and navigating by the stars may be of interest to more able children.

Discuss the possible reasons why Drake decided to go on this journey. (To obey the monarch; to attack the Spanish by plundering and making them a weaker nation; desire for riches; desire for fame and fortune; a sense of adventure; duty to God.)

Tell the children that they are now going to plot their own maps to show Drake's voyage, and to use their imagination to write a sailor's log.

Group activities

Activity sheet 1
This sheet is for children who need more support to read maps and follow routes. They have to use information from Generic sheet 2 to join up the seven stages on the map to plot Drake's voyage. They have to think carefully about stage 4 to 5, remembering that Drake does not go back round South America. Then they have to use information from Generic sheets 3, 4 and 5 to imagine they are a sailor with Drake. They have to write a paragraph, given guidance.

Activity sheet 2
This sheet is for children who can work independently. They have to use the information on Generic sheet 2 to join up the seven stages on the map to plot Drake's voyage. They have to add a date for each stage. Then they have to use information from Generic sheets 3, 4 and 5 to imagine they are a sailor with Drake. They have to write a diary entry for a sailor's day at sea.

Activity sheet 3
This sheet is for more able children. They have to use the information on Generic sheet 2 to join up the seven stages on the map to plot Drake's voyage. They have to make a key for the stages. Then they have to use information from Generic sheets 3, 4 and 5 to imagine they are a sailor with Drake. They have to write a detailed account of what life was like at sea.

Plenary session

Recap the main points on Drake's voyage. Starting with the map of Drake's circumnavigation of the world on Generic sheet 1, remind the children of the magnitude of his voyage – it took three years and no one really knew where he and his ship were travelling. Make a parallel with exploration in space today when going to the dark side of the Moon means that contact with Earth is lost for a few hours. Encourage the children to imagine the anxiety that brings for those involved. Emphasise that for Drake and his courageous sailors to return home successfully to retell their adventures was a momentous occasion in English history. Ask the children to give details of the conditions they travelled under again to emphasise what life at sea was like in Tudor times.

Ideas for support

For children who have difficulty recognising that the numbers on the map represent the order in which Drake completed his voyage, guide them from one point to the next, rather than looking at the map as a whole. Talk the child through the journey, adding descriptions to the facts on Generic sheet 2. Read the descriptions on Generic sheets 3, 4 and 5 to the child. Use a globe to help them.

More able children may want to research instruments from Tudor ships in more detail. The evidence from the *Mary Rose* exhibition is very helpful for this (see Useful resources on page 117).

Ideas for extension

Ask the children to imagine what it must have felt like to have been a sailor under Drake's leadership. Provide opportunities for drama, writing playscripts, extended writing and poetry.

With the children, create a display of three-dimensional ships sailing round a wall-sized map. On the map, ask the children to plot the route as the year goes by.

To bring the topic to life, use the *Mary Rose* website or visit the *Mary Rose* exhibition in Portsmouth. For details of life at sea, visit the *Golden Hinde* in London or the *Golden Hind* in Devon. (See Useful resources on page 117.)

Linked ICT activities

Using a drawing program such as *Dazzle* or Microsoft *Paintbrush* (see Useful resources on page 118), demonstrate to the children how to use the straight-line tool, the freehand drawing tool, the fill tool and the spray tool.

Using the internet, search for images of the *Golden Hind* and other Tudor ships. With these as a starting point, tell the children that they are going to create their own picture of a famous Tudor ship.

Start by showing the children how to create a background for their image by first drawing a line for the horizon and then filling in the sea and the sky. Save the background. Next work on the outline of the ship using the line tools. Save this second stage. For the third stage add some colour to the outline drawing and, using the drawing tools, add some detail to the picture. Save the final image.

Using a word processing program such as *Textease* or Microsoft *Word* (see Useful resources on page 118), show the children how to insert their saved picture onto a blank page. With the image on the page, they have to write their own brief description about their Tudor ship.

Drake's voyage

Drake's character

courageous
patriotic
great seaman
religious
courteous
generous
inspired loyalty
could be difficult to work with –
overbearing, ruthless,
fanatically Protestant

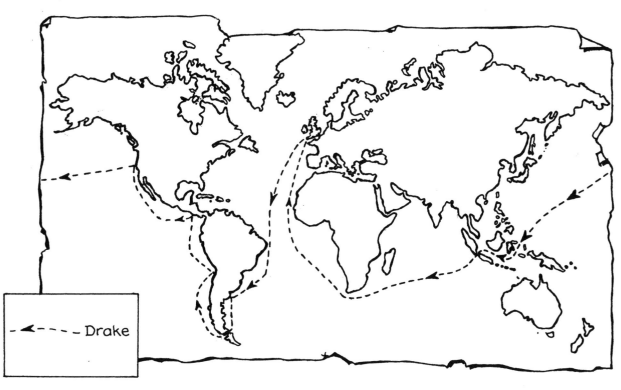

- ◄ - - - Drake

Drake's circumnavigation of the world

Drake's voyage

December 1577

Drake sets off from England with five ships.

Summer 1578

They reach the coast of South America; Drake abandons two ships.

Autumn 1578

Passes through the treacherous Straits of Magellan and loses a ship. Another ship returns home, leaving the renamed the *Golden Hind* to continue.

June 1579

Drake lands at New Albion and claims it for Elizabeth I.

Autumn 1579

Drake reaches the Spice Islands.

June 1580

He reaches the Cape of Good Hope, South Africa.

September 1580

Drake returns to Plymouth.

PHOTOCOPIABLE

Drake's voyage

The *Golden Hind*

- The name of this ship came from the golden hind emblem of Sir Christopher Hatton, who was a major shareholder in Drake's great voyage.
- The ship had three masts – fore (front), main (middle), and mizzen (stern).
- The big square sail in the middle was the main sail. The little one above was the topsail, sometimes furled (rolled up). It was the same for the fore mast. The mizzen mast had a triangular sloping sail called a lateen.
- The front of the ship was called the prow, where the sailors slept on the forecastle. There were then three decks, the lowest being called the main deck. At the other end of the ship (the stern), the quarterdeck rose from this main deck. At the very end of the stern, above the quarterdeck, was the poop deck, where the captain had his rooms.
- Cargo was kept in the hold in the middle under the main deck.
- Ropes were called rigging and they kept the masts up.
- The wooden bar that held the sail was called the yard.
- The crow's nest was the lookout post high up on the mast.

Drake's voyage

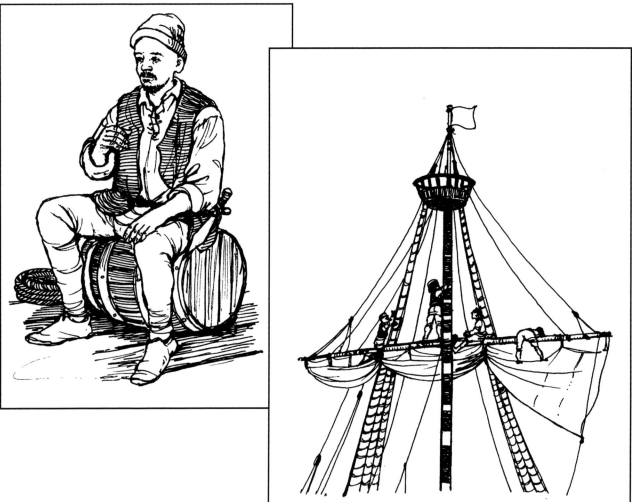

Sailors' work

The ship's crew were divided into two watches: one on duty and one asleep.

Their jobs were:

- to find out which way the wind was blowing and at what strength – if it was too strong, they had to take some of the sails down, but if it was only a breeze, they had to put more sails up;
- to keep the ship clean;
- to pump out any water;
- to mend sails;
- to mend ropes;
- to furl sails along the yard;
- to climb and check the rigging;
- to act as lookout in the crow's nest – looking for other ships and for land.

Drake's voyage

Life at sea

- The crew had to provide their own clothes.
- Officers slept in bunks while sailors slept on deck.
- Meat and fish were stored in salt.
- Bread and ship's biscuits always went mouldy, rotting in the heat and damp.
- Food was cooked in an iron box on a bed of sand in the front of the ship.
- Ships were full of lice, cockroaches and rats.
- Water was stored in treated barrels.
- Beer and cider were often drunk rather than water.
- The captain and his officers navigated using stars and compasses to turn the ship in the right direction. A cross-staff was used as a navigation tool to find the angle between the Sun at midday and the horizon. An astrolabe was used to measure celestial bodies in order to calculate latitude. (A sextant does the work of both these tools today.)

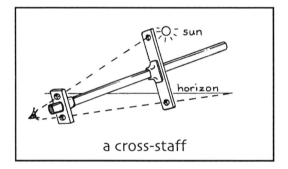

a cross-staff

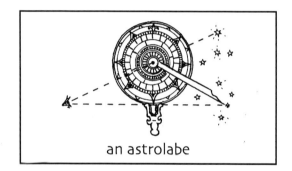

an astrolabe

- To measure the speed of a ship, a block of wood with a long line of rope securely fastened to it was thrown into the water. The rope was reeled out as the ship moved along. Using a sand timer, the sailors noted how much rope ran out after a certain length of time. They could repeat this exercise at different intervals and so begin to work out the ship's speed by comparing the results.

- To navigate using the stars, the captain would use a quadrant. This was a metal quarter circle with degrees marked along the rounded edge. At the right-angled corner hung a small weight known as a plumb line. The captain would aim the right-angled corner at a well-known star such as the North Star. The plumb line would hang vertically so the captain could read off the degrees on the quadrant. This number would help him to work out his position on a map, in degrees of latitude.

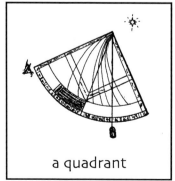

a quadrant

Drake's voyage

Join the seven stages of Drake's route around the world.
Use Generic sheet 2 to help you.
Think carefully before you join up points 4 and 5.

Clue: Drake goes west from North America to Australia, not back around South America.

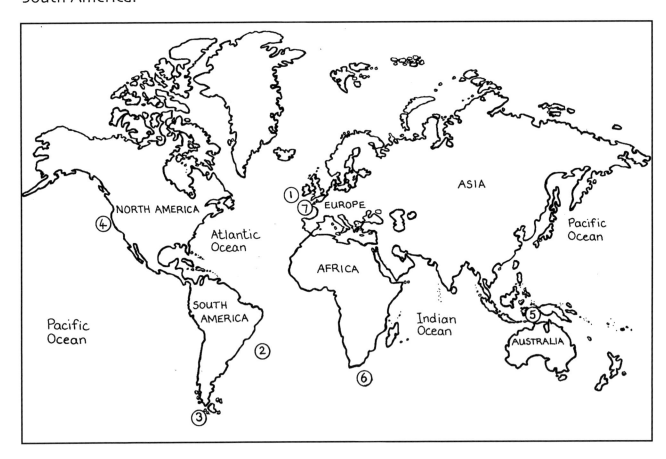

Imagine you are a sailor with Sir Francis Drake. Use Generic sheets 3, 4 and 5 to help you.

- What sort of work do you do?
- What sort of food do you eat?
- Where do you sleep?
- What do you drink?

On the back of this sheet, write a paragraph to answer these questions. Add any other information that you discover.

PHOTOCOPIABLE

Name _____

Drake's voyage

Join the seven stages of Drake's route around the world.
Use Generic sheet 2 to help you.
Next to each number, write the date when he reached that point.

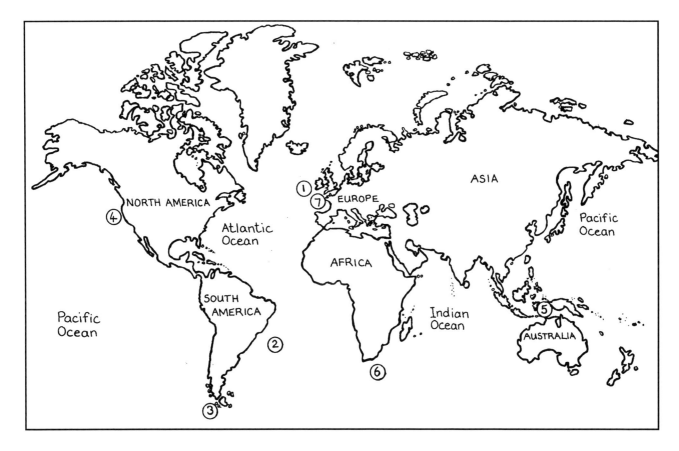

Imagine you are a sailor with Sir Francis Drake. Use Generic sheets 3, 4 and 5 to help you. Write a diary entry for a day at sea.

Name _____

Drake's voyage

Join the seven stages of Drake's route around the world.
Use Generic sheet 2 to help you.
Create a key for the stages.

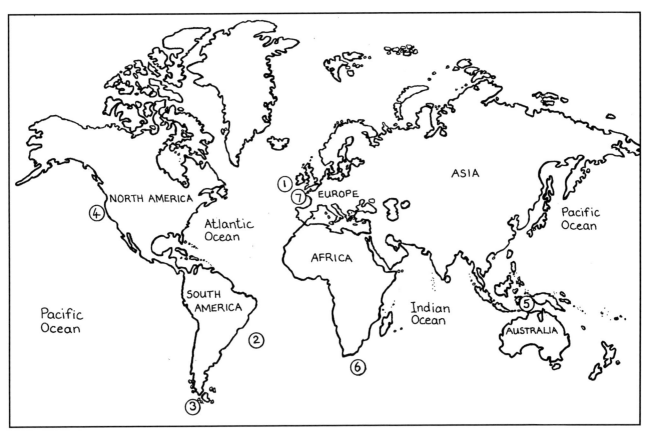

Key

Imagine you are a sailor with Sir Francis Drake. Use Generic sheets 3, 4 and 5 to help you.

On the back of this sheet, write a detailed account of what life at sea is like, including the work you have to do.

PHOTOCOPIABLE

Settlements in America

CHAPTER 10

TEACHERS' NOTES

Early colonisation

One of the main reasons for exploration in Tudor times was to take settlers to new countries to increase English influence abroad. In the 1570s and 1580s, North America was being considered as a good place for English settlements. Central and South America were occupied by the Spanish, but the north was still relatively untouched.

Sir Humphrey Gilbert (stepbrother of Sir Walter Raleigh) and members of his family took part in early colonisation efforts. In 1578, Gilbert was granted permission from Queen Elizabeth to attempt the colonisation of America. Gilbert is said to have believed that America was the lost continent of Atlantis. On 23 September 1578, he set sail from England with a large fleet, but an attack by the Spanish forced him to return home. Although this attempt failed, his stepbrothers, Walter and Carew Raleigh, then started to become interested in the exploration of America.

Gilbert made his second attempt in 1583, leaving Plymouth on 11 June with five ships. Four of these ships reached North America and Gilbert landed in St John's, Newfoundland, some time between 30 July and 3 August and took possession. Gilbert claimed the area for Queen Elizabeth I and started a colony. After two weeks in his new colony, Gilbert left to explore the harbours and creeks, and was then planning to travel back to England to record his claim. Although his men had encouraged him to travel in the *Golden Hind*, he sailed in the much smaller *Squirrel*. On 19 September 1583, the *Squirrel* sank near the Azores. All the crew drowned.

Sir Walter Raleigh

Walter Raleigh (see Generic sheet 1 on page 107) came to the notice of Queen Elizabeth in 1581 and for the next ten years was one of her favourites. In 1584, Raleigh was granted a licence to colonise America and came up with the idea of naming the new lands Virginia after Elizabeth, the so-called Virgin Queen. Later that year, on 13 July, Raleigh discovered Roanoke Island off the coast of the area now known as North Carolina (see Generic sheet 2 on page 108), and reported his finding back to the queen. The low, narrow island lies between the Outer Banks and the mainland. It was marshy land, protected from the worst sea gales. The queen, who knighted Raleigh on 6 January 1585, would not allow her favourite to back to Roanoke, but offered financial support for an expedition instead. The party that sailed from England in 1585 was under the command of Raleigh's cousin, Sir Richard Grenville. Seven ships, carrying 600 men, made up the expedition, half of the men being soldiers under the command of Ralph Lane. Also accompanying them was a scientific expert, Thomas Hariot, and a cartographer and watercolourist, John White.

Amerindians

Most evidence of the indigenous Amerindian way of life comes from the paintings of John White, who was briefly part of the English colony at Roanoke in 1585. His paintings of the Secotan people were published as engravings; they influenced the European concept of 'Indians' for the next 200 years. He copied pictures of the Florida Timucua with their traditional body tattoos (see Generic sheet 3 on page 109).

The homes of the Secotan were made from bent saplings, covered in bark and woven mats. All the homes were protected within a wooden palisade. The area had its own temple.

Eventually the Secotan were displaced by other Amerindian tribes and much of our knowledge of Amerindians comes from this later period. The story of Pocahontas (1595-1617) comes soon after the Roanoke experience. Fishing and hunting by the men provided a major part of their food. Carved wooden utensils have been found, but much of what we know is based on evidence from a later date.

The colony at Roanoke

When the colonists reached Roanoke they built cottages with thatched roofs, and a fort on the north of the island for defensive purposes. Initially, the local Amerindian islanders were friendly and helped Grenville and his men plant crops and catch fish. However, the Amerindians had few resources to spare when times got hard and they looked upon the settlers as rivals. Discord intensified when some of the Amerindians were kidnapped and held hostage in exchange for information. Things took a turn for the worse when in mid-1585, while Grenville was exploring the island and the nearby mainland, an Amerindian stole a silver cup from his ship. In retaliation, Grenville burnt the village of Aquascogok. This led to war between the local chief, Pemisapan, and the English settlers. The fighting was fierce and led to many deaths on both sides, including Chief Pemisapan.

By August 1585, the colonists were short of supplies and Grenville decided to return to England. He took with him a friendly Amerindian. Back home in Devon, Grenville dressed the Amerindian in English clothes and christened him Raleigh after his cousin. But the English climate was too damp and the Amerindian Raleigh died a year later.

Unfortunately for the colonists, Grenville's return was delayed and their situation was getting desperate. Then on 9 July 1586, Sir Francis Drake came to their rescue. He had dropped anchor near the island after destroying the Spanish colony of St Augustine in the West Indies, and offered to take the colonists home to England.

A second attempt

A few days later, Richard Grenville arrived back with supplies, but found the settlement deserted. He left 15 men and two years' provisions on Roanoke to keep an English presence there, while he went back to England to prepare a second attempt to colonise the island. In July 1587, the colonists returned to Roanoke Island, but this time the settlers included women and children. On 18 August, their number grew by one when John White's daughter, Elenora Dare, gave birth to a girl, Virginia, the first English child to be born in the New World.

Unfortunately, the Amerindian islanders showed little friendliness to the newcomers. Apart from some bones of a possibly murdered man, there seemed to be no other traces of the fifteen men left behind by Grenville. An Englishman, George Howe, was then attacked and killed by the Amerindians while out exploring. The settlers retaliated by attacking the town of Dasamonquepeuc, burning houses and killing many of those living there.

Things were steadily getting out of hand, but calmed down with the help of two Amerindian guides, Manteo and Wanchese.

A strange disappearance

On 27 August 1587, John White, who was now governor of the colony, left his family and 114 colonists and sailed for England to fetch supplies. He also promised to return with a back-up fleet, which would hopefully include Sir Walter Raleigh. Due to the English war against Spain, which resulted in the Spanish Armada, it was to be 17 August 1590 before he returned. He was puzzled to find the island deserted – no Amerindians, no English. The colony had disappeared and, apart from the word 'Croatan' carved on a post, there were no clues as to where they had vanished. Had they gone to the nearby Croatan Island? Although both English and Spanish search parties looked for clues to the colony's disappearance for many years, the mystery has never been solved.

Even with a setback such as this, England was still eager to gain a colonial foothold on the North American continent, but now it was the turn of James I to support the colonists. Humphrey Gilbert's son, Raleigh Gilbert, continued the colonising efforts of the family, and in 1606 was one of eight explorers to be given permission and a grant of money by the king to set up two colonies. Captain John Smith was one of the founders of the settlement at Jamestown, Virginia. He was one of 105 settlers who sailed from England on 19 December 1606, landing on 26 April 1607. By 24 May 1607, Jamestown had been established as the first permanent settlement in North America, with Smith as the colony's leader.

Raleigh Gilbert sailed from England on 31 May 1607 and arrived in what is now the state of Maine on 1 August 1607, but this settlement was not to be a success.

Colonisation continues

The interest in colonisation continued throughout James I's reign. In 1620, the Pilgrim Fathers established the first settlement in New England. By the 1770s, 13 colonies had been established. During the reign of George III, these American colonies finally won their independence in the American Revolution of 1775–83.

Settlements in America

LESSON PLAN

History objectives (Unit 19)

- To apply their knowledge and understanding of settlement in England to a new context – settlement in America.
- To understand the difficulties that faced the settlers in Roanoke.
- To find out about the ways of life of indigenous people before colonisation.
- To consider how the English settlers viewed the indigenous people.
- To explore the causes of the failure of the colony.

Resources

- Generic sheets 2–4 (pages 108–110)
- Activity sheets 1–3 (pages 111–113)
- A globe or atlas

Starting points: *whole class*

Ask the children to find the coast of America with Virginia on it, on a globe or in an atlas and then ask them to find Britain. Ask questions such as:

- Which ocean lies between the two countries?
- How would you get from Britain to America today?
- How long would you stay there for?

Discuss transport systems such as jumbo jets, ocean liners and hot-air balloons. Help the children to grasp the magnitude of the journey. Some of their relatives may fly back and forth quite regularly.

Take the children back in time to the first English people wanting to settle in America. Explain that there were already indigenous Amerindians living there. Use the maps on Generic sheet 2 to point out the location of Roanoke and show the children Generic sheet 3 to give them some idea of what an Amerindian village would look like. Using the teachers' notes for guidance, go through the points on Generic sheet 4 with the class.

Tell the children that they are going to complete a crossword about life at Roanoke, and then compare life on Roanoke Island with life in Tudor England.

Group activities

Activity sheet 1
This sheet is for children who need more support. After they have completed the crossword, they have to imagine (using Generic sheet 3) what it must have been like for the first English settlers to live among the indigenous Amerindians. They need to recall their work on Tudor housing, food and clothing for comparison. On the back of the sheet, they have to write a paragraph about why they think the settlement failed.

Activity sheet 2
This sheet is for children who can work independently. After they have completed the crossword, they also have to imagine (using Generic sheet 3) what it must have been like for the first English settlers to live among the indigenous Amerindians. They need to recall their work on Tudor housing, food and clothing for comparison. They have to make a chart showing differences between the settlers' and the Amerindians' ways of life. They also have to write a paragraph about why they think the settlement failed.

Activity sheet 3
This sheet is for more able children. After they have completed the crossword, they also have to imagine (using Generic sheet 3) what it must have been like for the first English settlers to live among the indigenous Amerindians. They need to recall their work on Tudor housing, food and clothing for comparison. They have to write a paragraph about why they think the settlement failed. They also have to imagine what it was like for the Amerindians to have their home invaded by the English settlers. They have to present their findings as a poem, a newspaper report or a play.

Plenary session

Discuss with the children the Roanoke experience using their activity work as a basis for reflection. Look at the experience from the point of view of the Amerindians as well as the settlers. Guide the children to think about the families left behind in England who lost loved ones in Roanoke. Finish by asking them why the Roanoke settlement failed. Encourage the expression of different opinions.

Ideas for support

For children who find it difficult to look analytically at pictures, ask questions such as 'What are the houses made from?', 'How big do you think they were?' and 'How many rooms were in each house?' Refresh their memory on Tudor housing using the illustrations in Chapters 5 and 6.

Give the children clues about food by pointing out that Roanoke was an island in a large river. Ask whether they think the fish would be cooked on fires. Ask them to describe the clothes and tattoos of the Amerindians – could they imagine someone in Tudor England dressing like that?

More able children can benefit from researching Roanoke on the internet.

Ideas for extension

Using the illustration of Amerindians on Generic sheet 3, encourage the children to compare the clothing with that of Tudor people. Ask them to research clothes and their practical uses through reference books, CD-Roms and the internet.

Challenge the children to design a 3-D replica Amerindian village of Roanoke, using the illustration of the village on Generic sheet 3.

Linked ICT activities

Using Microsoft *PowerPoint* or another multimedia presentation package, show the children how to create different effects with text and images. Show them how to create a series of slides and run their own slide show presentation.

Tell the children that they are going to create their own presentation to show to the rest of the class about settlements in America. They have to create a presentation in no more than six slides. Use Generic sheet 4 as an example of how to write simple short paragraphs about the different stages in the settlement. Encourage use of the internet to search for further information and images.

Settlements in America

Sir Walter Raleigh

Settlements in America

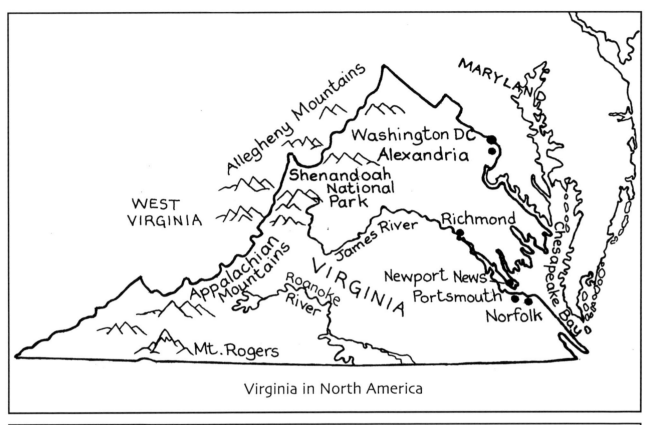

Virginia in North America

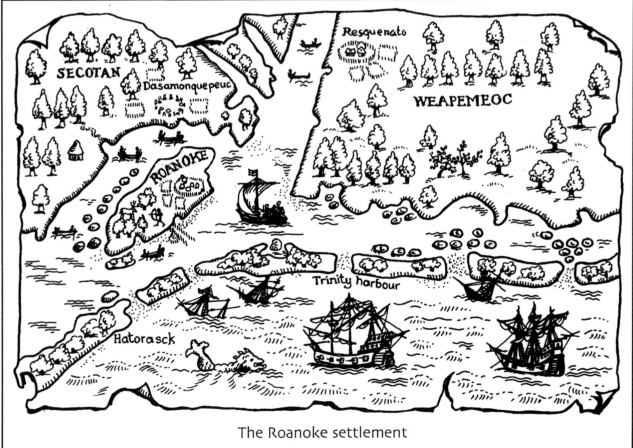

The Roanoke settlement

Settlements in America

An Amerindian village

Amerindian man and woman

Settlements in America

In 1578, Humphrey Gilbert was given permission by Elizabeth I to set up a colony in America. He made the first attempt late that year but was unsuccessful.

Gilbert's second attempt was made on 11 June 1583 when he left Plymouth with five ships. He reached Newfoundland in North America towards the end of July, claimed the area for Queen Elizabeth and started a colony. Gilbert died in September 1583 when his ship the *Squirrel* sank near the Azores.

Walter Raleigh had also been given permission by Elizabeth I to colonise America, and he came up with the idea of calling these new lands Virginia after Elizabeth, the Virgin Queen. Raleigh discovered Roanoke Island while exploring the region off the coast of North Carolina. The year was 1584.

A party of settlers sailed for Roanoke in 1585. Raleigh's cousin, Richard Grenville, led them. When they reached Roanoke the settlers built cottages and a fort. The local islanders, the Amerindians, were friendly to start with, but later fought against the English. Grenville returned to England in August 1585 for more supplies.

Grenville was delayed back in England and the settlers were getting desperate. Luckily, on 9 July 1586, Francis Drake came to their rescue. He had dropped anchor near Roanoke and offered to take the settlers home. They happily accepted.

In July 1587, the colonists returned to Roanoke Island, but this time with women and children as well. On 18 August, Virginia Dare was born on Roanoke. She was the first English child to be born in America.

In August 1587, John White, the governor of the colony, sailed back to England to fetch supplies. When he returned to Roanoke Island in 1590, the colony had disappeared completely.

Name _____

Settlements in America

*

```
[crossword grid]
1 □□□□□□□
  2 □□□□□□□□□
      3 □□□□□□
4 □□□□□
        5 □□□□□□□□□
      6 □□□
        7 □□□□□□□□□□□
```

Solve the clues using the word bank. Fill in the answers on the grid.
Write the word that reads down from the *.

1. Humphrey G_____ was allowed to set up a colony in America.
2. On 11 June 1583, five ships left P_____ for America.
3. Walter R_____ discovered Roanoke Island.
4. The local islanders were called A_____
5. In July 1587, the c_____ returned to Roanoke.
6. Francis D_____ came to the rescue of the settlers in 1586.
7. Virginia was named after Queen E_____

```
┌─────────────────────────────────────────────────────┐
│                      WORD BANK                        │
│    Amerindians      Gilbert       Plymouth    Raleigh │
│    Drake            Elizabeth      colonists          │
└─────────────────────────────────────────────────────┘
```

Imagine what it was like for the first English settlers to live among the
Amerindians. Use Generic sheet 3 to help you. Remember what Tudor houses were
like in England, the sort of clothes the Tudors had and the food they ate. On the
back of this sheet, write about:

- how different you think it was to live in Roanoke compared with England
- say why you think the colony at Roanoke may have failed.

Settlements in America

*

Solve the clues. Fill in the answers on the grid.
Write the word that reads down from the *.

1. In 1578, Elizabeth I gave Humphrey _____ permission to set up a colony in America.
2. On 11 June 1583 five ships left _____ for America.
3. Walter _____ discovered Roanoke Island.
4. The local islanders were called _____
5. In July 1587, the _____ returned to Roanoke.
6. Francis _____ came to the settlers' rescue in 1586.
7. Virginia was named after Queen _____

Imagine what it was like for the first English settlers to live among the Amerindians. Use Generic sheet 3 to help you. Remember what Tudor houses were like in England, the sort of clothes the Tudors had and the food they ate.

On the back of this sheet, make a chart to list the differences between the English and the Amerindian ways of life. Your columns should be headed 'English' and 'Amerindian'.

On the back of this sheet, write a paragraph to say why you think the colony at Roanoke may have failed.

PHOTOCOPIABLE

Name _____

Settlements in America

Solve the clues. Fill in the answers on the grid. Write the word that reads down from the *.

1. In 1578, this man was given permission by Elizabeth I to set up a colony in America (surname needed).
2. Five ships left this English port on 11 June 1583.
3. The surname of the man who discovered Roanoke Island.
4. The local islanders were given this name.
5. The name that describes the group of people who returned to Roanoke in July 1587.
6. This man rescued the settlers in 1586 (surname needed).
7. This queen had Virginia named after her.

Imagine what it was like for the first English settlers to live among the Amerindians. Use Generic sheet 3 to help you. Remember what Tudor houses were like in England, the sort of clothes the Tudors had and the food they ate.

On the back of this sheet, write a paragraph about how different it must have been to live in Roanoke. Then write why you think the colony at Roanoke may have failed.

On a separate sheet, write a poem, a newspaper report or a play about how Amerindians would feel about English settlers invading their homeland.

Answers

Chapter 3

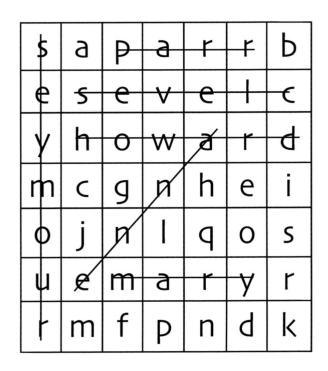

Chapter 4

Henry VIII married Catherine of Aragon to gain the friendship of Spain.

Henry VIII married Anne Boleyn to get a son.

Henry VIII married Jane Seymour to get help from the Protestants.

Henry VIII married Anne of Cleves to get Germany's help against Charles V.

Henry VIII married Catherine Howard to get the support of the Catholics.

Henry VIII married Catherine Parr as a companion in his old age.

Chapter 10

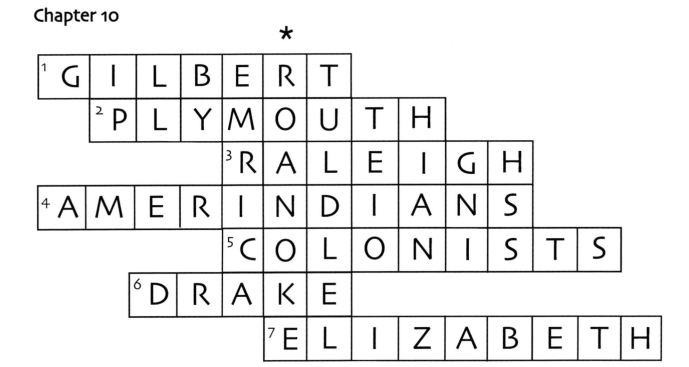

Glossary

Chapter 1

alliance: an agreement between two or more countries

Catholic: part of the Christian Church with the Pope as its head

court: a king or queen's advisors

dynasty: the hereditary line of kings and queens from the same country

monarch: a king or a queen

power: the authority of important people

Protestant: all parts of the Christian Church that are not Catholic or Orthodox

state: the land occupied by the governing ruler and his or her people

Chapter 2

alliance: a formal agreement between two or more countries to help each other

chronological: events arranged in the order that they happened

court: any place where a king or queen lives

courtier: a member of a royal court

monarch: the king or queen

power: the authority of the monarch

state: land occupied by the governing ruler and his or her people

Chapter 3

betrothed: engaged to be married

dispensation: permission from the Pope to do something against Church law

execution: death by being beheaded or hanged

papal bull: a signed document from the Pope

treason: the act of not being loyal or faithful to one's monarch or country

Chapter 4

arranged marriage: marriage decided by parents

Catholic Church: part of the Christian Church with the Pope as its head

divorce: the end of a marriage

heir: someone who is going to inherit a title, property or the throne

parchment: 'paper' made from sheepskin

politics: the governing of a country

Pope: head of the Catholic Church

Protestant: someone who disagreed with the teachings of the Catholic Church; Protestants in England recognised the monarch as head of the Church

religion: practice of beliefs

vellum: 'paper' made from calf-, goat- or deerskin

Chapter 5

affluent: rich, wealthy

andirons: the iron stand on which log fires were built

architecture: the style and design of a building

comfit: a sweet

daub/plaster: clay, lime, straw, cow dung and water used to fill in walls

exterior: the outside

gables: the triangular end of the wall and roof

garderobe: toilet

great hall: a large main room often two storeys high with a balcony

interior: the inside

inventory: a list of possessions

long gallery: upper room going the length of the building

merchant: someone who trades a variety of goods from many places

parlour: the living room

pewter: mixture of tin and lead used to make plates and drinking vessels

platter: a large plate for serving food

rush nips: candleholders for rushes soaked in fat

storey: the floor level of a building

wainscoting: wood panelled walls

wattle: interwoven hazel twigs

Chapter 6

common: land that was available for everyone to graze their animals on

deserving poor: those who were poor in Tudor times through no fault of their own – for example, the lame, the blind, widows, orphans

disability: inability to work due to physical causes

ducking stool: a chair extending over a river on which women were made to sit and then ducked into the water as a punishment

enclosure: the practice of putting hedges around land to keep sheep and cattle in safety, carried out by landowners

hooker: a thief who used a long pole to hook things through rich people's windows

scolds: women who told lies

stocks: wooden beams with holes for the heads and arms (and sometimes legs) of wrongdoers to be fastened into whilst other members of the public enjoyed throwing over-ripe fruit and vegetables at them as a form of punishment

Chapters 8 and 9

astrolabe: a navigation instrument

bow: the forward end of a ship

circumnavigate: to sail (or fly) completely round

colony: a group of people who set up home a long way from their homeland but keep contact with it

cross-staff: a navigation instrument

crow's nest: the lookout post high up on the mast

discover: to be the first to find something

explore: to travel to unknown lands

forecastle: where the crew slept at the front end of the ship

furl: to roll up (the sails)

latitude: the position (in degrees) north or south of the equator

main sail: the big sail on the middle mast

mizzen mast: the mast at the stern end

poop deck: above the quarterdeck where the captain had his rooms

prow: the front end of the ship also known as the bow

quadrant: an instrument for measuring the altitude of stars

quarterdeck: the deck above the main deck at the stern end

rigging: the ropes

stern: the rear of the ship

topsail: the smaller sail above the main sail

voyage: a journey

yard: the wooden beam to which the sail was attached

Chapter 10

Amerindian: a native person of North America

indigenous people: people native to any country or area

New World: America

palisade: a protective wooden fence built around a group of homes

settlement: a group of people who have come together to live in a country

Useful resources

Places to visit

- **Anne of Cleves' House, East Sussex**: part of her divorce settlement from Henry VIII. Sussex Past Education, Barbican House, 169 High Street, Lewes, E Sussex BN7 1YE. Tel 01273 405734; fax 01273 486990; www.sussexpast.co.uk/aoc/aoc.htm
- **Hampton Court Palace, Surrey**: The Education Booking Coordinator, Historic Royal Palaces, Barrack Block, Hampton Court Palace, East Molesey, Surrey KT8 9AU. Tel 0870 752 5190; fax 0208 781 9533; www.hrp.org.uk/webcode/hampton_home.asp
- **Hever Castle, Kent**: childhood home of Anne Boleyn. The Estate Office, Hever Castle Ltd, Hever, Edenbridge, Kent TN8 7NG. Tel 01732 865 224; group bookings email bookings@hevercastle.co.uk; www.hevercastle.co.uk
- **Little Moreton Hall, Cheshire**: Britain's most famous and first timber-framed moated manor house. Little Moreton Hall, Congleton, Cheshire CW12 4SD. Tel 01260 272 018
- **The *Golden Hind*, Brixham Harbour, Devon**: replica ship offering educational visits. Tel 01803 856 223; email postmaster@goldenhind.co.uk; www.goldenhind.co.uk
- **The *Golden Hinde*, London**: replica ship on display on the Thames. Built in 1973 it is a reconstruction using Elizabethan techniques. It has travelled more miles than the original ship, going to San Francisco to commemorate Drake's claim for Elizabeth I as well as circumnavigating the world. It is now used for educational purposes. Contact: The *Golden Hinde*, St Mary Overie Dock, Cathedral Street, London SE1 9DE. Tel 08700 118 700; www.goldenhinde.co.uk
- **Tower of London:** the 'royal fortress on the Thames'. Contact HM Tower of London, London EC3N 4AB. Information line: Tel 0870 756 6060
- **Windsor Castle:** the largest occupied castle in the world; exhibitions include famous Tudor portraits. Online ticket office for group bookings on www.royal.gov.uk/output/Page557.asp

Museums and exhibitions

- ***Mary Rose* exhibition, Portsmouth:** the only 16th-century warship on display anywhere in the world. Contact the Chief Executive, College Road, HM Naval Base, Portsmouth PO1 3LX. Tel 0239 275 0521; fax 0239 287 0588; group bookings 0239 283 9766; www.maryrose.org
- **Museum of London:** tells the story of London from prehistory to the present day, including galleries of Tudor and early Stuart London. Contact Museum of London, London Wall, London EC2Y 5HN. Tel 0207 600 3699; fax 0207 600 1058; info@museumoflondon.org.uk
- **National Maritime Museum, London:** excellent information on Drake's and Raleigh's voyages. Park Row, Greenwich, London SE10 9NF. Tel 0208 858 4422; www.nmm.ac.uk
- **National Portrait Gallery, London**: excellent portraits of all Tudor monarchs. St Martin's Place, London WC2H 0HE. Tel 0207 312 2473/4/5/6; fax 0207 312 2464; www.npg.org.uk
- **Totnes Museum, South Devon**: Tudor pottery, panelling and furniture in an Elizabethan merchant's house. 70 Fore Street, Totnes, Devon TQ9 5RU; Tel 01803 863 821
- **Weald and Downland Open Air Museum, Chichester, West Sussex:** a good place to visit to see a reconstruction of a Tudor farm. Tel 01243 811 459; email coursebookings@wealddown.co.uk; www.wealddown.co.uk

Books

Wilson, L (1995) *Daily Life in a Tudor House.* London: Hamlyn.
Shuter, J (1995) *The Poor in Tudor England*. Oxford: Heinemann.

Websites

Focus on Tudors:
www.backtowhen.com how people lived, dressed, cooked and entertained in Tudor England
www.brims.co.uk/tudors/index.html NGfL-approved site written for 7–10 year olds

www.britishexplorers.com/woodbury/raleigh/
html factual information for teachers covering
colonisation of America and a painting of Raleigh
from 1600
www.goldenhind.co.uk replica of the *Golden Hind*
in Devon
www.goldenhinde.co.uk replica of the *Golden
Hinde* in London
www.hevercastle.co.uk Anne Boleyn's childhood
home
www.hrp.org.uk/webcode/hampton_home.
asp Hampton Court Palace
www.library.yale.edu/MapColl/wrld1607.gif
Yale University Map Collection includes the 1607
world map
www.maryrose.org Mary Rose Trust site with
easily accessed information about the *Mary Rose*
and Tudor life; has a KS2 section
www.mcn.org/2/oseeler/drake.htm factual
details on Drake
www.museum-london.org.uk Museum of
London
www.nationalcenter.org/ColonyofRoanoke
information on Roanoke
www.nationalgeographic.com excellent site for
old maps including the 1565 map:
http://plasma.nationalgeographic.com/mapmachin
e/plates.html?id=501565
www.nmm.ac.uk National Maritime Museum:
excellent information on Drake's and Raleigh's
voyages
www.npg.org.uk National Portrait Gallery:
excellent portraits of all Tudor monarchs may be
downloaded
www.nps.gov/fora/test/gilbert.htm
information on Gilbert and Roanoke
www.royal.gov.uk/output/Page557.asp
Windsor Castle
www.toweroflondontour.com Tower of London
virtual tour
www.schoolhistory.co.uk/primarylinks/Tudor
times.htm interactive site for KS2 children
www.sussexpast.co.uk/aoc/aoc.htm Anne of
Cleves' House
www.theheritagetrail.co.uk for details of Tudor
homes
www.wealddown.co.uk Weald and Downland
Open Air Museum including a virtual tour

Other useful history/research sites:
www.encyclopedia.com good research tool

www.historyonthenet.co.uk aimed at teachers
and children, with timelines, A-Z of history, games
and useful links
www.educate.org.uk/teacher_zone/classroom
/history excellent resource site for extra lesson
material
www.primaryresources.co.uk/history/history/
htm general information for teachers
www.royal.gov.uk the British monarchy's own
website is easy to navigate by more able children
www.teachingideas.co.uk/history/contents.
htm full of ideas

ICT resources

CD-Rom
Microsoft *Encarta*

Videos
BBC Primary History: Tudors and Stuarts, BBC video,
www.bbcshop.com
The prince and the pauper (1979)
The six wives of Henry VIII, David Starkey's Channel
4 series (2002) on video and DVD,
www.c4shop.co.uk
Henry VIII and his six wives, 1972 film based on the
BBC series, Castle Communication Video
Henry VIII and his six wives, 1971 BBC series of six
plays, BBC Video, www.bbcshop.com

TV programmes
What the Tudors and Stuarts did for us, BBC TV series
by Adam Hart-Davis; book of the series published
by Boxtree, London, 2002

Resources recommended for linked ICT activities

Software:
Dazzle Granada Learning/SEMERC, Granada
Television, Quay Street, Manchester M60 9EA. Tel
0161 827 2927; www.granadalearning.com
Numberbox Granada Learning/SEMERC,
Granada Television, Quay Street, Manchester M60
9EA. Tel 0161 827 2927;
www.granadalearning.com
Textease 2000 Softease Ltd, Market Place,
Ashbourne, Derbyshire DE6 1ES. Tel 01335 343
421, fax 01335 343 422; www.softease.com

Websites:
Chapter 1
www.burbage-jun.leics.sch.uk/tudors/index/
index_page.htm
Chapter 2
www.burbage-jun.leics.sch.uk/tudors/index/
index_page.htm
www.maryrose.org
www.tudorhistory.org

Chapter 3
http://atschool.eduweb.co.uk/40903026a/java
/cube1/sixwives.htm
http://englishhistory.net/tudor.html
www.historylearningsite.co.uk/anne_boleyn.
htm
www.larmouth.demon.co.uk/sarah-
jayne/wives/wives.html
www.toweroflondontour.com/kids

Chapter 5
www.canterburytrust.co.uk/schools/primary/
tudor.htm
www.historic-uk.com/HistoryUK/England-
History/TudorChristmas.htm
www.nettlesworth.durham.sch.uk/time/tlife.
html
www.standrcp.fsnet.co.uk/tudors.htm

Chapter 7
www.school2000.org/tudors.html
www.standrcp.fsnet.co.uk/tudors.htm

Chapter 8
www.heatonmanor.newcastle.sch.uk/lrc/lower
/history/tsfr.htm

Chapter 9
www.nettlesworth.durham.sch.uk/time/tships.
html

Digital camera:
Digital Dream 'L'Elegante' digital camera for
children: TAG Learning. Tel 01474 357 350; fax
01474 537 887; www.taglearning.co.uk